155.413

CHILDREN'S COGNITIVE DEVELOPMENT

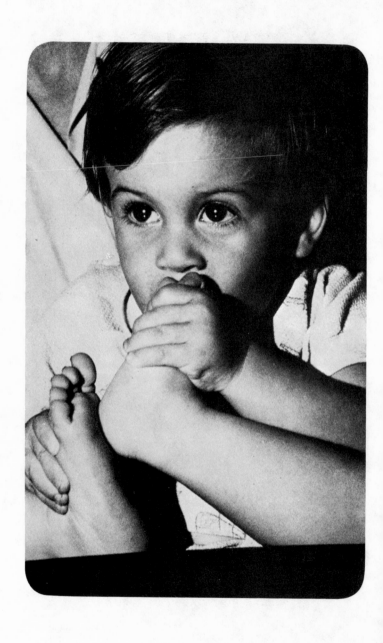

CHILDREN'S COGNITIVE DEVELOPMENT

SECOND EDITION

RUTH L. AULT
Davidson College

New York   Oxford
OXFORD UNIVERSITY PRESS
1983

Library of Congress Cataloging in Publication Data

Ault, Ruth L.
  Children's cognitive development.

  Bibliography: p.
  Includes index.
  1. Cognition in children.   I. Title.
BF723.C5A9 1982   155.4'13   82-3529
ISBN 0-19-503183-0   AACR2
ISBN 0-19-503184-9 (pbk.)

The author acknowledges the kind permission of authors and publishers to reproduce material from the following sources:

R. Gelman, "Conservation acquisition: A problem of learning to attend to relevant attributes." *Journal of Experimental Child Psychology*, 1969, 7, p. 174. Copyright © 1969 by Academic Press. Reprinted by permission.

P. R. Kingsley and J. W. Hagen, "Induced versus spontaneous rehearsal in short-term memory in nursery school children." *Developmental Psychology*, 1969, 1, p. 41. Copyright © 1969 by the American Psychological Association. Reprinted by permission.

M. A. Kreutzer, C. Leonard, and J. H. Flavell, "An interview study of children's knowledge about memory." *Monographs of the Society for Research in Child Development*, 1975, 40(1, Serial No. 159), pp. 9, 11, 25, 29, 43, 49. Copyright © 1975 by the Society for Research in Child Development, Inc. Reprinted by permission.

A. A. Milne, *The house at Pooh Corner*. N.Y.: E. P. Dutton, 1956, pp. 86, 94. Reprinted by permission of the following publishers: (a) E. P. Dutton & Co., Inc. Copyright 1928 by E. P. Dutton & Co., Inc. Renewal, 1956, by A. A. Milne. (b) The Canadian Publishers, McClelland and Stewart Limited, Toronto. (c) Associated Book Publishers, Ltd., London.

A. A. Milne, *Winnie-the-Pooh*. N.Y.: E. P. Dutton, 1954, pp. 86-87. Reprinted by permission of the following publishers: (a) E. P. Dutton & Co., Inc. Copyright 1926 by E. P. Dutton & Co., Inc. Renewal, 1954, by A. A. Milne. (b) The Canadian Publishers, McClelland and Stewart, Limited, Toronto. (c) Associated Book Publishers, Ltd., London.

P. A. Ornstein, M. J. Naus, and C. Liberty, "Rehearsal and organizational processes in children's memory." *Child Development*, 1975, 46, p. 822. Copyright © 1975 by the Society for Research in Child Development, Inc. Reprinted by permission.

Illustrations by Fred Winkowski

Printing (last digit): 9 8 7 6 5 4 3 2 1

Printed in the United States of America

PREFACE TO THE FIRST EDITION

Since I had a purpose and readership in mind when I wrote this book, I ought to share that information with you, the reader. This book was designed as a supplement to college courses in child development, particularly as taught in Psychology departments, but also including Educational Psychology, Family Life, and Nursing departments in which an unspecialized course in child development is taught. The target audience is, therefore, undergraduate with not necessarily more than an Introductory Psychology course as a prerequisite. Why read a supplement at all? A glance through child psychology texts provides the answer. A majority of such texts emphasizes the child's physical and social development, relegating cognitive development to a secondary role. Often a single chapter covers both Piaget's theory and information about standardized intelligence testing. The topics of memory and perception are frequently missing or presented disjointedly. In few cases is there any attempt to compare or contrast the Piagetian approach with the approach of the non-Piagetian experimental child psychology (called the *process approach* in this book). This book, then, seeks to remedy that situation. It has been kept short enough to function as a supplement to full-length child psychology texts but is long enough to fill in the bare sketch of cognitive development painted in the primary texts. Although other cognitively oriented supplements exist, they are primarily introductions to Piaget's theory alone and are deeper treatments than is desirable for general introductory courses.

This text has a dual orientation, presenting both Piaget's theory and the research efforts of experimental child psychologists who have cognitive, but not necessarily Piagetian, interests. Such an orientation requires the presentation of research results in somewhat greater detail than is common at the introductory level. Having taught child psychology for several years, I know that the mention of research can produce sheer panic in some students. Puzzled by complicated research designs and arcane statistical analyses, introductory (and many advanced) students shy away from experimental psychology. My intention is to bring research findings to the reader in an intelligible and as nontechnical a fashion as possible. For me, that meant describing enough about an experiment that the reader would understand both its results and their significance. This contrasts with the usual treatment of listing one-sentence summaries of the results, which end up being viewed as isolated facts to be memorized. An intelligible presentation also meant excluding statistics, ignoring aspects of experiments that were tangential to the point being discussed, and avoiding the technical jargon of experimental psychology. The advantage over a book of readings that reprints journal articles is clear. For the advanced reader, reference citations indicate sources of further information: original sources in the case of journal articles and other books in the case of Piaget's theory.

The reader should also note that this book has been liberally sprinkled with footnotes. Like all good footnotes, those in this book are tangential to the basic information of the main presentation. Some provide slightly more technical information that the reader may wish to pursue. Others are what I consider to be humorous asides.* I hope the reader will read them.

I also hope that the reader will find this book both useful and enjoyable, for those were my two goals in writing it. Although it is certainly not a layman's guide to parenting or educating children, it is intended to be helpful to anyone who has contact with the younger members of our species. The underlying philosophy is that a basic understanding of normal cognitive development should help make interactions with children more sensible and, consequently, more pleasant.

Before I started this work, I read the prefaces of many other books. I was continually skeptical of the acknowledgment sec-

---

* Or snide remarks, depending on one's perspective.

tion, wondering how the author ever cajoled (or conned) so many of his colleagues into reading endless drafts of the manuscript. Having now written this book, I am amazed at, and eternally grateful for, the number who helped me. Encouragement came from faculty, students, secretaries, and friends alike. In particular, I wish to thank Donna Gelfand, Donald Hartmann, Joen Lessen-Firestone, Cindy Cromer, Christine Mitchell, and Lizette Peterson for their highly useful and detailed comments on manuscript drafts. Irwin Altman, David Dodd, and Marigold Linton helped prepare me for my initial contact with publishers (a bewildering business for novices). Janine Seely and Judie Turner served as able typists. Friends and their children provided many of the delightful anecdotes I have recounted here, but I suspect they wish to remain anonymous.

Finally, I wish to thank my husband. Not only did he suffer through the normal trials and tribulations of a spouse whose partner is writing a book, but he also tolerated such unreasonable demands as thinking up stories to illustrate some point I wished to make (usually by counterarguing that *he* did not have many years of experience studying children and mine *ought* to suffice). After laughing hysterically at my initial sketches, he drew the figures for the manuscript draft submitted to the publisher.* He also cheerfully read draft after draft, providing insightful comments and encouragement. In return for these considerations, he demanded that I become a successful author and support him in the style to which he wanted to become accustomed. A fair bargain to my way of thinking.

Salt Lake City   R.L.A.
January, 1976

* His laughter was quite justified, I might add.

PREFACE TO THE SECOND EDITION

The timing for a second edition of a book is not difficult to predict. The author must lose the reluctance to tamper with a finished product, be sufficiently embarrassed over ill-written passages, think of new (and better) ways to express the old material, and have new material to present. The first three conditions need no further elaboration. As for the new material, readers will find that this edition has expanded coverage in three of the five previous chapters. In Chapter 2, which deals with Piaget's theory, research involving class inclusion, conservation, and Formal Operational tasks is treated more thoroughly in order to evaluate the theory more critically. In addition, the chapter expands upon the stage aspects of Piaget's theory. In Chapter 3, all three major processes (perception, memory, and the generation and testing of hypotheses) are considered in greater depth, and the research concerning them is updated. The process called evaluation has been dropped entirely since it does not seem to have stood the test of time. In Chapter 5, the educational implications of Piaget's theory and of the process approach receive much greater treatment.

My own research into the educational implications of both psychological approaches was significantly enhanced by visits to the Circle Children's Center at the University of Illinois Chicago Circle campus and to the Eliot-Pearson Child Development Institute at Tufts University. I am grateful to Maureen Ellis and David Elkind for facilitating those visits. In addition, I wish to thank the North Carolina National Bank for the faculty research support provided to Davidson College which enabled me to make those trips. I would also like to thank Christine Mitchell for discussions of Piaget and memory, Brian Nash for proofreading and checking references, and my colleagues at Davidson College for their encouragement. Marcus Boggs, editor at Oxford University Press, has been a gentle persuader, provider of good meals, and friend. I owe more than I can express to my husband for his unlimited support of both this project and my career.

Davidson, N.C.   R.L.A.
February, 1982

CONTENTS

CHILDREN'S COGNITIVE DEVELOPMENT

1

INTRODUCTION

Four-year-old Susan was asked where she got her name. She answered, "My mommy named me." "What if your mother had called you Jack?" "Then, I'd be a boy." To many children, names embody certain other characteristics; if one has a boy's name, then one must have other features making one male. Susan also claimed that if the name of the sun were changed and it were called the moon, "then it would be dark in the daytime."

A three-year-old girl, with a gleam in her eye, approached a plant. Her mother cautioned her not to touch it. "Why not?" "Because you might hurt it." "No, I won't, 'cause it can't cry." She associated crying with hurting and denied the possibility of the one without the other.

When asked to define "priceless," an eight-year-old guessed that it meant "something that's for free." Children tend to interpret words and expressions literally (see Figure 1-1).

These are just some of the numerous examples of how children's thinking is different from the thinking of adults. The study of cognitive development examines these differences in thinking and the causes of these changes as children grow older. The practical implication of cognitive development is

3

"Curiosity killed the cat."

clear. How a child thinks, and how his* thinking changes as he develops, has an obvious impact on his behavior at home and on what he learns at school. In addition to the practical significance, studying children's thinking can be fascinating and fun. Although the expression beginning "out of the mouths of babes" usually refers to the honesty with which children speak,

---

* Of course half of all children are "shes" and not "hes," but the English language is not well-suited to referring to a single child without assigning sex. In this book, references to a child as "he" are presumed to include "she." Similarly, parents and teachers will generally be labeled female with all due apologies to fathers and male instructors.

4

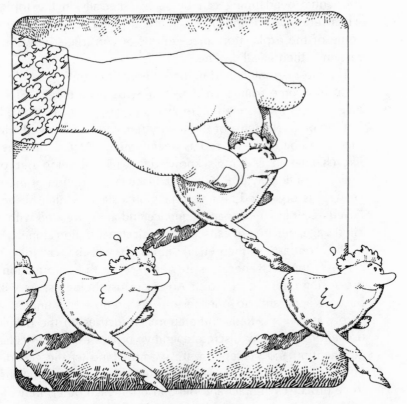

"Billy caught 40 winks."

Figure 1-1. Proverbs and metaphors conjure up childish mental images

it also serves to remind us that children say what they think and that their thinking can be amusingly different.

The purpose of this book is to describe briefly the course of cognitive development. The description will take two forms because psychologists have studied the development of thinking from two theoretical perspectives. Although initially the two approaches were viewed as incompatible, each approach has been modified by the arguments of the other so that now substantial overlapping can be seen, especially in the topics which are studied and in the methods used to study them. Some of the explanatory mechanisms or constructs, however, remain in theoretical dispute.

The most complete and unified theory of cognitive development has come from Jean Piaget, a Swiss psychologist. Since Piaget's writings spanned more than 50 years, his ideas evolved, but the basic elements of the theory remained unchanged. His theory can be characterized as tracing the *qualitative* or *stage-like* changes in children's knowledge which develop out of their interactions with their world. Piaget's description of these changes is organized around four global stages which he believed occur in an invariant sequence and are correlated with a child's age, but are not caused by physical maturation alone.

The contrasting theoretical approach will be called the *process* approach because it stems from the information-processing tradition of North American psychologists. As will become apparent, no one person has proposed as unified a theory as Piaget's. Rather, the approach focuses on the development of relatively discrete cognitive processes, in particular (a) attention and perception, (b) memory, and (c) the generation and testing of hypotheses. While acknowledging that the three processes interact and depend upon each other, individual researchers have typically focused on just one process. The basic theoretical position is, therefore, less coherent, but it can be characterized as tracing the quantitative, nonstage, changes in children's problem-solving skills or information-processing capacities. The changes may or may not occur in any particular sequence. They are, to some extent, correlated with age, but not caused by age alone.

ASSUMPTIONS

Despite the differences which should already be apparent, these two approaches share many features including two fundamental assumptions. These cognitive assumptions distinguish them from theories based on the behavioral or S-R approach.

THE ACTIVE CHILD

We assume that children are *active* rather than passive participants in their own development. This assumption means that children are not merely passive recipients of whatever environmental stimulation happens to impinge upon them. Rather, they actively seek certain types of stimulation and avoid others. For example, a child may look at the bars of his crib rather than the middle of the plain mattress. He may focus on his mother's eyes instead of her ears. He may turn his head toward the sound of his mother's voice, but not toward the window when the lawn mower passes by. In being active, children help to determine what behaviors they will exhibit. A 10-month-old may babble sounds like *maah, mmmah, mahmah, may,* and *mey,* until he can produce the particular sound he desires or until he masters and controls his own behavior.

This position does not deny the importance of environmental stimuli in shaping children's behavior. Consider again children's babbling. Research has shown that the early babbling of American babies (around 10 months old) is indistinguishable from that of Chinese babies, but the sounds of those children a few years later are quite distinctive (Atkinson, MacWhinney, & Stoel, 1970). American babies learn to speak English, not Chinese. The environment must be influencing children to result in this language shaping. By the same token, children contribute to the process too. They exercise some choice regarding how much time to spend babbling in contrast to some other activity and whether to babble the *ma* syllable or the *da* one.

The assumption of an active child implies that children inherently try to make sense out of their environment. Experiences in the environment are classified, organized, and related to each other because that is the nature of the mind. These

7

mental manipulations create problems to be resolved, and children seek new experiences to help solve them. As soon as they have figured out the solution (to their own satisfaction), they will turn their attention to other matters. In other words, children are active because they are intrinsically motivated to learn about their world. How do children decide which of the numerous problems confronting them to solve? The *moderate novelty principle* proposes that a person's attention is attracted to events that are mildly different from the old. Events that are completely familiar are boring; events that are too discrepant from the familiar are either unintelligible or frightening. Hence children and adults tend to turn to moderately novel problems.

THE INTERACTIONIST POSITION

When a behavior is universal, occurring in virtually every human being, one could postulate that the behavioral sequence is innate—a wired-in aspect of our nervous system. This position, called *nativism,* occupies one extreme of the spectrum. The people who advocate nativism are frequently called maturationists because they believe that behavior stems from physical maturation of the organism living in a minimal environment (one containing oxygen and food). The other extreme of the spectrum is *empiricism,* which postulates that some experiences are so pervasive that all people are exposed to them in every known culture. The empiricist position is advocated by environmentalists (not to be confused with conservationists) since they believe that behaviors are learned as a result of experience with the environment, given a minimally working physical body (an intact brain and spinal cord). In between the two extremes is a wide range of positions reflecting varying degrees of *interaction* between the forces of mother nature (maturation) and of nurture (learning). Interactionists maintain that the biological and cultural aspects of a person's life are so

8

intertwined that it is difficult, or even meaningless, to try to separate the impact of these two forces.

Clearly, infants are born with some innate behavioral sequences. All healthy infants cry when pricked by a pin. And some cultural experiences are so pervasive that all children are exposed to them. For example, all infants are fed by someone else, or they do not survive. Most behavior, however, results from a combination of inherent predispositions and environmentally determined influences. The interactionist position is advocated by nearly all psychologists who study cognition, and both Piaget's theory and the process approach fit into this category.

Corresponding to the three positions (maturation, environmental experience, and their interaction) are three terms, each of which describes a change in behavior over time. *Growth* is that change which arises from physical maturation of the body. *Learning* is change due to contact with some environmental experience. *Development,* the most general change, is a function of both maturation and experience. Thus, when a change in behavior is labeled as growth, learning, or development, the cause of the change has been implicitly stated as maturation, environmental experience, or their interaction, respectively. The reader should recall these implicit causes whenever these terms occur. The title of this book, *Children's Cognitive Development,* reflects its interactionist position.*

METHODS OF STUDY

To study children's thinking, cognitive psychologists rely on two major methods: observations and experiments. In a naturalistic observation, the investigator watches and records what-

---

* Titles such as *Children's Learning* and *Studies in Cognitive Growth* were purposely avoided for two reasons: they might imply a learning or maturation orientation which would not be intended, and two excellent books already possess those titles, by Stevenson (1972) and by Bruner, Olver, and Greenfield (1966), respectively.

ever happens as a child goes about his daily activities. If a naturalistic observation is to be thorough, the investigator must have daily access to the subjects for long portions of the day. Since even close family friends are usually unwilling to tolerate such intrusions into their lives, investigators typically observe their own children. That increases the chance that the observer will be biased in recording and interpreting events. Even the most objective observers occasionally yield to the temptation to regard their own children as little angels. It is also difficult for the observer to refrain from participating in, and thereby influencing, the course of events. Rarely can an observer remain passive when the child's curiosity leads him to investigate the properties of matches. The enormous time demands of the observational method usually limit the study to a few children. The observer then cannot determine whether some phenomenon is peculiar to the few children in the observation or whether it has more widespread generality. Conclusions drawn from small sample observations are, therefore, open to the criticism that they are not applicable to broad ranges of children. Piaget's early writings (1951, 1952, 1954) were just such naturalistic observations of the development of his own three children. His later works (e.g., Piaget & Inhelder, 1973), however, were experiments in the same tradition as the process approach research.

In an experiment, often conducted in a laboratory, children are asked to perform certain tasks as specified by the investigator. Their performance is assessed according to some predetermined standard or relative to the performance of other children. Experiments are purposely designed to be less biased because the person who tests the children is typically unfamiliar with any of them and often does not even know the purpose of the experiment. Experiments permit greater generality because large numbers of children can be tested. An additional advantage stems from systematic manipulations of the environment. Scientific statements of cause and effect can only be made when the experimenter has controlled the presence or absence of some treatments and has obtained systematic effects as a result. In observations, the investigator can describe factors as they occur, but deciding between alternative causal explanations such as maturation, past learning, or a current stimulus requires measuring and contrasting groups of children. Experiments can suffer, however, from artificiality and narrowness of scope. The laboratory setting establishes a contrived situation that may induce children to behave in an unusual manner, and because only one small facet of the child's thinking processes is studied at a time, the interrelations between processes are difficult to investigate. Observations are much richer in portraying the whole child.

Experiments and observations each provide data that the other cannot; each is a valuable method for adding to our knowledge about children. Corresponding to the observational and experimental methods are two ways to organize the collected information about children. Since a naturalistic observer typically studies all facets of the same child's behavior as that child develops, it is not surprising that the results of these observations tend to be organized by *ages* or *stages*. All of the child's cognitive skills are observed for relatively long periods of his life, such as infancy or adolescence. An experimentalist, on the other hand, usually studies the performance of many groups of children, often of different ages, on a small set of related tasks during relatively brief sessions. These techniques suggest an organization by *process*. One particular problem-solving skill, for example, memory, is discussed for all ages before the next skill, for example, perception, is examined.

Neither organization is completely satisfactory for presenting cognitive development. If information is presented according to the age of the child, then the reader lacks a concise understanding of the development of a process. If the child's problem-solving skills are discussed as units (first one skill and then another), the reader has a poor comprehension of the child's capacities at any one moment in time. To adopt one organizational framework unfortunately relegates the other to a subsid-

11

iary status, but like the observational and experimental methods, both the stage and process organizations offer valuable contributions to the study of cognitive development.

OVERVIEW OF THE REMAINING CHAPTERS

Chapter 2 presents the theory of Jean Piaget. It begins with the theoretical constructs he proposed to account for developmental change. Then the chapter sketches the four major stages of cognitive development. Piaget's writings were rich and compelling descriptions of very real children and they have stimulated a considerable amount of research. The chapter includes a small sample of that research and its implications for the theory. Chapter 3 presents a sample of the data obtained primarily through laboratory experiments derived from the information-processing tradition. Three problem-solving processes are examined: perception, memory, and hypothesis testing. Since no one theory fits all these pieces together, the account may seem disjointed, but it is a valid and valuable representation of the facts we know about children's thinking.

Because results are more understandable when the experimental procedures are also understood, brief descriptions of many experiments are presented in Chapters 2 and 3. The reader without much background in psychology should rest assured that the presentations are simplified and technical jargon has been avoided as much as possible. For the more advanced reader, reference citations indicate the original sources to which the reader can turn for more detailed information. Some of the similarities and differences between Piaget's theory and the process approach are highlighted in Chapter 4. The two approaches are now more similar than they were 10 or 20 years ago, as researchers of each perspective have tried to incorporate the ideas and data of the other, but important differences remain.

The fifth and final chapter is an attempt to make the preceding chapters relevant to parents and educators. It exemplifies how adults can evaluate problem-solving tasks in terms of the demands placed on the child's capacity to think. The underlying philosophy of this book is that each child is unique, has an individual rate of development, and has an individual set of needs. Hence, no one list of specific suggestions will suit the various situations that parents and educators meet daily in their interactions with children. Chapter 5, therefore, is not a comprehensive manual on child rearing or child educating. Nor can it be a compendium of useful suggestions for the distraught parent or teacher. Instead, it proposes that adults create their own list of solutions based on an assessment of the child's current level of cognitive development and of the task demands.

In essence, the approach is to deny two popular ideas: the concept of the "average" child and the "correct" way to handle children. The average child is as mythical as the unicorn. No person has ever seen one. His characteristics are assigned according to whatever statistical average results from measuring a sample of children. Real children have unique clusters of abilities, some above and some below the average. What is a description of the average child will not necessarily describe any one particular child.

Similarly, if each child is unique, then no one way of handling a situation can be uniformly right or wrong. Wise advice givers must always hedge their bets. They rarely have as much information about the specific situation as the advice seeker and so cannot make as informed a judgment. They can, however, tell the advice seeker what factors might be weighed in the decision. That is the function of this book's final chapter.

It is always difficult to decide how to limit the topics under consideration, especially since the maxim "Everything always relates to everything else" is particularly appropriate for the psychology of human organisms. The determining factors in this book are a combination of personal bias, traditional lines of psychological inquiry, interest for the reader, and availability of research findings, but not necessarily in that order.

13

2

PIAGET'S THEORY OF
COGNITIVE DEVELOPMENT

Piaget's theory concerns the development of intelligence, that is, how children construct knowledge of the world and how they put that knowledge to use. Piaget wrote extensively on various aspects of children's cognitive development, but this brief introduction cannot do full justice to such a comprehensive and complex theory. Only a few of the most basic terms and assumptions underlying Piaget's theory can be explained, and only a cursory look can be taken at the developmental stages that he proposed. More detailed information about Piaget's theory can be obtained from many excellent books, including Brainerd (1978), Flavell (1963), Furth (1969), and Ginsburg and Opper (1979).

DEFINITION OF TERMS

According to Piaget, intelligence has a functional aspect, which is how the cognitive system works, and a structural aspect, which is the knowledge the system produces.

14

FUNCTIONS

Piaget (1970) has said that one cannot understand his theory unless its biological basis is examined first. He "borrowed" two functions from biology—organization and adaptation—to explain both stability and change in development. Neither organization nor adaptation is directly observable; rather, each is inferred from a person's activity.

Organization refers to the tendency of behaviors or thoughts to become clustered into systems of related behaviors or thoughts rather than to remain isolated. For example, infants have several individual behaviors such as grasping, sucking, and looking, which at first function independently. If someone places an object in an infant's palm, the baby will grasp the object. If the object appears in front of his eyes, he will look at it. But the infant who has not yet organized these two behaviors will not perform them simultaneously. With development, that is, with maturation and experience, the infant will come to look at things he grasps and grasp things he looks at. Organization happens spontaneously; it is not something which takes conscious or deliberate effort. Piaget considered organization to be a mechanism of cognition because it is a basic biological principle and because he observed the combining of behaviors and thoughts into higher-order, smoother-functioning units.

The second biological mechanism, *adaptation,* consists of two complementary processes: *assimilation* and *accommodation.* Assimilation is the process of incorporating new pieces of information into old ways of thinking or behaving. Let us suppose that an infant knows how to grasp, bite, and shake various objects that are in his crib. For the first time, he is confronted with a new object, such as a stuffed doll. He will try to understand this new object by applying what he already knows how to do; he will grasp, bite, and shake the doll (probably

15

disassembling it in the process). Thus, part of the child's adaptation to a new experience is to assimilate it.

The other part of the child's adaptation is to accommodate to the object's unique features. Accommodation involves modifying some elements of the old ways of thinking and behaving or learning new ways that are more appropriate to the new object. Grasping can be modified by gripping tightly or loosely as a function of an object's weight. One of the properties of stuffed dolls is that they can be rubbed. Once the child learns to rub the doll, accommodation has occurred.

Another example of the usefulness of the concepts of assimilation and accommodation can be seen in the preschool child's early attempts to count. As Gelman (1979) described it,

> It is hard, if not impossible, to explain [young children's] tendency to count *on their own* without the notion of assimilation. A 2½ year old may say "2-6" when counting a 2-item array and "2-6-10" when counting a 3-item array. The fact that young children invent their own count lists can be explained if we assume that counting principles . . . are guiding the search for (or assimilation of) lists in the environment. Likewise, the shift from the use of idiosyncratic count lists to the conventional ones . . . makes sense if we recognize the workings of accommodation. [P. 3, italics in the original]

Piaget (1970) proposed that both assimilation and accommodation occur simultaneously whenever the child adapts to an environmental stimulus. He modeled these processes after biological systems such as digestion, in which food is assimilated by breaking it down into a form which the body can use, while at the same time the body accommodates to the food by secreting enzymes and contracting muscles. In both digestion and cognition, assimilation and accommodation always occur, but the particular balance between them can vary from situation to situation. Feedback from the environment is one important factor in determining which process is more influential. Other important factors include the extent to which the new stimulus

16

situation differs from previous ones and the kinds of behaviors or thoughts the child already has. Let us consider again the example of the child who has been given the stuffed doll. When he applies his old behaviors, he finds that grasping and shaking the doll do not produce very interesting noises. Biting a stuffed doll can be unpleasant (depending on the stuffing), so the child looks for new things to do with it and eventually comes upon rubbing. Accommodation has thus played a larger role than assimilation.

For a contrasting example, let us suppose that the child has been given rattles before, with handles one-half inch or less in diameter. Then he is presented with a new rattle with a handle one-inch in diameter. For the most part, the child will assimilate the new rattle, applying the old behaviors of grasping and shaking it. He will have to accommodate only slightly. He must open his hand wider in order to grasp it, hold on harder, and shake with more force to produce any noise. In his adaptation to the new stimulus of a one-inch handle, assimilation has played a larger role than accommodation.

Piaget stated that one of the forms of adaptation takes definite precedence over the other in two situations. In make-believe play, the child's behavior is predominantly assimilation. The child ignores the "realistic" features of an object and responds to it as if it were something else. In many nursery schools, for example, a corner of the classroom is set up for playing house. Children can be seen sweeping the floor, washing dishes, and setting the table. One child straddles a broom, pretending to be flying. The broom's sweeping capabilities are ignored while the child interacts with it as if it had wings. While we can look at such play as evidence of creativity, the child is not learning anything about brooms as sweeping instruments. Imitation, on the other hand, is primarily accommodation. The child learns new behaviors by imitating someone else's behaviors. When a boy observes his mother pet a dog and then imitates and pets the dog, he is accommodating to it. The dog could not be a completely novel object, however, because the boy needs a framework to which he can connect the newly imitated behavior. Accommodation will not occur if the behavior to be imitated is too novel. Each time a child accommodates more than he assimilates, he adds to his repertoire of behaviors and becomes a bit more mature. In other words, advances in cognitive development are greater when accommodation plays a larger role than assimilation because the child's repertoire of behavior expands. Assimilation is still very important, though, for the child understands new objects by applying old patterns of behaving to them. As Piaget (1970) has said, "Assimilation is necessary in that it assures the continuity of [mental] structures and the integration of new elements to these structures" (p. 707).

Assimilation and accommodation are, in one sense, opposing forces. Assimilation tries to maintain the child's current status and force change upon the external situation, while accommodation tries to maintain the external situation and force change on the child. Such tension between two forces must reach a balance, or the system will fail to thrive. Consequently, Piaget proposed a self-regulating mechanism, *equilibration*, which coordinates the actions of assimilation and accommodation. Cowan (1978) likened equilibration to a steam engine's governor "which shuts down the engine temporarily when the steam pressure builds up, and then allows the engine to switch on again" (p. 25). This analogy emphasizes that the regulatory mechanism is a property of the system (hence, self-regulatory) and not something imposed on it from outside stimulation. Piaget (1970) described equilibration as "a set of active reactions of the [child] to external disturbances" or to disturbances created by inner reflections (p. 725).

STRUCTURES

The structural aspect of Piaget's theory refers to the system of knowledge children construct out of their actions (first, physical and later, mental) with the environment. This system of knowledge takes on two forms: schemes and operations.

A *scheme* is an organized pattern of behavior. All of us engage in behavior patterns, or habits, which form part of our daily routine. Although we may never repeat any action exactly the same way, there is a similarity to the actions, and it is possible to recognize the critical, defining elements of the behavior pattern. To say that a child is sucking, for example, certain minimal criteria must be met. The cheeks and lips of the mouth must move in and out rhythmically in a drawing action, and some object, such as a thumb or nipple, is usually in the mouth. Other movements, such as the mouth opening and closing repeatedly, are the essential elements of other schemes, such as biting. In sucking, it does not matter whether the child's right thumb or left thumb is in his mouth, or whether he brought his thumb to his mouth after scratching his cheek or after brushing hair out of his eyes. The essential ingredients of the scheme are the sucking movements.

But more than just these common movements are implied in the definition of a scheme. The definition includes the idea that the scheme will be used because it is available to be used. Recall that in discussing assimilation we said that the child would grasp, bite, and shake a stuffed doll because those were schemes he already had. Assimilation occurs when old schemes are applied to new events.

The feature of schemes that highlights their importance in Piaget's theory is that by applying the schemes to various objects, the child can build up knowledge. Bottles and thumbs can be grouped together as objects-which-can-be-sucked, and they can be differentiated because one object often leads to food in the mouth and the other does not. Thus, from observing physical responses, such as an infant grasping a rattle and a bottle, Piaget inferred an underlying cognitive structure. The tendencies to grasp objects and to know objects as graspable are not, themselves, directly observable.

The other type of structure is an *operation*. Operations are more difficult to understand because they are not tied to behavior in as straightforward a manner as schemes. Operations are inferred from some commonalities children exhibit when they solve a particular set of problems. We will consider this in more detail in later sections; for now, operations can be defined by two characteristics: (a) they are mental, in-the-head representations and (b) they are reversible. Reversibility refers to the capacity to undo or compensate for one mental action by taking a different mental action and arriving back at the beginning state. Reversibility distinguishes operations from other types of mental activity such as imagining and perceiving.

The structural and functional aspects of Piaget's theory are closely interwoven. First, because of the principle of organization, all the elements in a structure are interrelated. One element cannot be changed without influencing the others. Second, each act of assimilation and accommodation transforms a structure, so structures appear dynamic and changeable rather than static. Third, structures develop from simple to more complex forms. Finally, Piaget emphasized the active role of the child in constructing structures. Structures are not imposed on the child from external stimulation or experience, nor are they merely preformed in the genetic makeup to unfold with maturation. Rather, "the construction of structures is mainly the work of equilibration" (Piaget, 1970, p. 725). Equilibration is an active reaction or compensation to some cognitive discrepancy, but it does not reestablish a prior balance point by discounting some of the conflicting data. Instead, equilibration involves building a new balance which will allow the cognitive system to "integrate disturbances into wider and more powerful structures" (Lovell, 1979, p. 16).

By oversimplifying a bit, one can say that Piaget's theory accounts for cognitive development in terms of the development of structures, from the schemes of the infant to the schemes plus operations of the adult. Piaget said that this occurred in four major time divisions, variously called stages or periods (although in some articles [e.g., Piaget, 1970], the mid-

20

dle two periods are combined). We shall adopt the terminology that *stages* characterize the smallest units of change which meet certain criteria such as being qualitative (rather than quantitative) and occurring in an invariant sequence. *Periods* are broader time blocks incorporating several stages within them. A fuller discussion of the requirements for a stage theory occurs at the end of this chapter.

The first of the four periods is the Sensorimotor Period, beginning at birth and lasting 1½ to 2 years. During this period, children have only schemes. The Preoperational Period, from 1½ to 6-7 years, is a transition between the predominant use of schemes and the use of operations. Children begin to use such mental representations as symbols and language, but these are not true operations. In the Concrete Operational Period, from 6-7 to 11-12 years, children have some true operations, but these can only be applied in concrete, physically real situations. Finally, in the Formal Operational Period, from adolescence through adulthood, operations have developed to the point where they can be applied to abstract and hypothetical problems. Table 2-1 summarizes these periods.

Here as elsewhere in the book, ages associated with the various periods and stages are meant to be rough approximations only. In addition to describing stages and periods of general cognitive processes, Piaget described stages in the development of some specific abilities. While we shall be concerned primarily with the general periods, brief descriptions of specific

TABLE 2-1

FOUR PERIODS OF COGNITIVE DEVELOPMENT

Period	Approximate Age Ranges
Sensorimotor	Birth–1½-2 years
Preoperational	1½-2–6-7 years
Concrete Operational	6-7–11-12 years
Formal Operational	11-12–through adulthood

abilities (such as object permanence) will be presented as well.

THE SENSORIMOTOR PERIOD

The first period of development is called *Sensorimotor* because children solve problems using their sensory systems and motoric activity rather than the symbolic processes that characterize the other three major periods. Children's knowledge about objects comes from their actions on them. At this point we need to pause briefly to examine some perceptual-motor capabilities of the newborn. Then we shall return to Piaget's theory and see how the perceptual-motor system is used in the Sensorimotor Period.

Although infants may appear completely helpless at birth, many of their senses are functioning. From the moment of birth, when their eyes are open, infants can see. The muscular control of eye movements is not very precise, and they have sharp focus only for those objects 9-10 inches from their faces because the muscles controlling the curvature of the lenses are not fully developed. Nevertheless, newborns can perceive color and shape when there is good contrast to the surrounding visual pattern. Since infants startle in response to loud noises and quiet in response to soft voices, we know that the sense of hearing functions from birth. Babies cry when stuck with a diaper pin and fuss when too hot or too cold; thus we know that the senses of pain and temperature are operative. Touching, stroking, and rocking typically soothe a fussing infant, leading to the conclusion that the sense of touch and bodily posture cues are meaningful to newborns. Finally, controlled experiments with a baby's reactions to different odors and tastes have permitted us to learn that the sense of smell works immediately from birth but taste discrimination is delayed for several days. Thus infants are capable of receiving stimulation through the many sensory modalities they are born with.

22

In addition to perceiving stimulation, newborns are capable of reflexive behavior. Reflexes are responses that all normal members of a species exhibit after a particular type of stimulation. Typically, psychologists consider reflexes unlearned. That is, the species-specific response occurs the very first time the stimulus is contacted, and it is not necessary for the organism to observe anyone else making that same response or to be taught. Examples of reflexes in adults are the knee jerk when a doctor's hammer strikes the patella, and the constriction of the eye's pupil in response to bright light.

Some infant reflexes clearly have survival value. Among these are the rooting reflex, the sucking reflex, and the grasping reflex. The rooting reflex helps the infant locate his mother's breast for feeding. When a baby's cheek is stroked, he will turn his head toward the side that was touched and open his mouth. Then, when anything touches the infant's mouth, he begins sucking. Together the rooting and sucking reflexes ensure that with a little help from his mother, the infant can obtain food. The grasping reflex is triggered by any object placed in the palm of the baby's hand. His grasp is strong enough that the infant can be pulled from a lying to a sitting position just by grasping an adult's fingers. The grasping reflex was probably significant in evolution when babies were transported by clinging to their mothers. Newborns also have reflexes for yawning, hiccoughing, sneezing, coughing, withdrawing an arm or leg if pricked with a pin, and so on.

Other reflexes indicate how mature the infant is. The Babinski reflex, named after its discoverer, seems to be an indicator of the state of the central nervous system. When the outer sole of the infant's foot is stroked, the infant fans his toes apart and arches his foot. Between about four and six months of age, the Babinski reflex disappears, and the infant now curls his toes downward in response to the sole stroke, just as adults do. If an infant still has a Babinski reflex after his first half year of life, damage to the central nervous system may be indicated.

Finally, there are reflexes whose functions are currently unknown. One example of this is the "walking" reflex. If infants are held upright with their feet lightly touching a surface such as a table top, they will step in alternation, as if walking. These reflexes disappear, but the behaviors return later under voluntary control.

With the reflexes and sensory capacities outlined above, infants are ready to begin interacting with their world. Their reflexes allow their sensory systems to contact many objects. As they look at, hear, touch, taste, and smell things, they acquire valuable information about their environment. Before this interaction takes place, infants do not know whether things are hot or cold, hard or soft, smooth or rough, sharp or blunt, tasty or ill-tasting. They do not even know what belongs to their own bodies and what is part of the external world. They soon find out, though, that biting their own toes causes pain whereas biting most other objects does not.

The amount of information infants must learn is truly enormous, and they have only their reflexes and sense organs with which to begin the process. Since the infant's reflexive systems are not as precise or discriminating as they could be, Piaget observed that one of the first significant changes to occur in infant behavior is the modification of some of these reflexes. These changes characterize the first of the six stages within the Sensorimotor Period.

STAGE 1: MODIFICATION OF REFLEXES

When children are born, the sucking reflex is an automatic response to anything placed in the mouth. The reflex at first functions equally well to the stimulus of fingers or pieces of clothing as it does to nipples of bottles or breasts. During the first month of life, however, the sucking reflex is modified, enabling hungry infants to suck more quickly and vigorously for milk while simultaneously enabling them to reject nonfood substances. When they are no longer hungry, infants can reject food but will still suck on toys or pacifiers. The reflex thus becomes both more efficient and more voluntary. In other words, infants learn to recognize objects by sucking on them and then can choose whether to suck or not.

In a similar manner, the rooting reflex first becomes more efficient, turning the head in precisely the proper direction for a given stimulus, and then drops out as more voluntary movements replace it. These voluntary head-turning movements arise from a combination of factors, including a maturing neuromuscular system and a conditioning process in which hunger, the presence of mother, and being held in a particular position are paired with the rooting and sucking reflexes.

Not all reflexes change in the Sensorimotor Period or, indeed, even in a person's lifetime. Pupil constriction to bright lights and withdrawal of a limb when pinpricked remain virtually unchanged. Nevertheless, those reflexes which do change demonstrate the significant changes in the first stage of the Sensorimotor Period.

STAGE 2: PRIMARY CIRCULAR REACTIONS

The second stage of the Sensorimotor Period has been called the stage of Primary Circular Reactions. During this time, if the infant's random movements lead, by chance, to an interesting event, the infant will attempt to repeat the behavior. The term *circular reactions* refers to the circularity or repetitive aspects of the behavior. An example of a primary circular reaction might be thumb sucking. The infant's thumb accidentally falls into his open mouth, triggering sucking, but then falls out. The infant then attempts to get his thumb back into his mouth so that the interesting event, sucking, can be repeated. The adjective *primary* refers to the fact that the interesting activity involves only the infant's own body. If there is any purpose to a circular reaction, it may be to practice a scheme, in this case, sucking; or there may be no demonstrable purpose at all. In any case, there is no intention to suck the thumb to find out what thumbs are like. Such investigatory intent is hypothesized to occur only at later stages in the infant's development.

STAGE 3: SECONDARY CIRCULAR REACTIONS

The Secondary Circular Reaction Stage follows (logically enough) the Primary Circular Reaction Stage. In this third stage of the Sensorimotor Period, infants still exhibit circular reactions (repeating interesting chance-occurring events), but now the repetitions involve events or objects in the external world, secondary to the infant's body. Piaget (1952) described an incident in which his son waved his arms, thereby swinging some balls which had been suspended above the crib and attached by a string to one hand. After observing a series of arm waves followed by intense stares at the swinging toy, Piaget concluded that his son acted for the purpose of repeating an interesting event. It might be argued that the pleasure of seeing the swinging toy caused such excitement in the baby that his arms waved, which accidentally resulted in the toy swinging again, which in turn excited the baby to swing his arms once more, and so forth. Piaget rejected this explanation because he noticed that the hand which was not connected to the string stopped moving. When Piaget changed the hand tied to the string, his son changed the arm he waved. Thus, intentionality can be inferred because of the refinements that occurred in the waving.

Even though infants in the Secondary Circular Reaction Stage know there is a connection between their behavior and the interesting events, these infants still have several cognitive deficiencies. Their behavior is not fully intentional, in the sense that the goal was discovered by accident. It is only after the interesting event has occurred that the infant desires it. In addition, their behavior is aimed solely at reproducing the prior event; they are not yet inventing new behaviors.

26

STAGE 4: COORDINATION OF SECONDARY REACTIONS

In stage 4, children can combine two or more previously acquired schemes to obtain a goal. The name of the stage is derived from this new achievement: children coordinate several of their secondary circular reactions. One frequently cited example from Piaget's observations (1952) involves his son reaching for a matchbox Piaget was holding. Piaget held a pillow in one hand and behind it he held the matchbox, thus presenting an obstacle in front of a goal. He observed his son strike the pillow to displace it and clear the way to grab the matchbox. By putting the previously acquired striking and grabbing schemes together in a coordinated manner, the child overcame an obstacle and reached the goal. In earlier stages, the child might have given up his attempts to grab the matchbox as soon as the obstacle was imposed, or he might have been distracted into striking the pillow repeatedly. What is new about this stage is the child's continued orientation toward a specific goal. In the sense that only previous behaviors are joined together, however, there is no novelty. That accomplishment comes in the next stage of development.

STAGE 5: TERTIARY CIRCULAR REACTIONS

The Tertiary Circular Reaction Stage is the fifth stage in the Sensorimotor Period. As the term *circular reactions* implies, events are still repeated, but the child has progressed to the point of actively seeking novelty. Actions are no longer repeated in exactly the same manner from trial to trial, as was done in earlier stages. Now children purposely vary their movements to observe the results. Infants perform actions as if they were learning about the properties of objects as objects or actions as actions, not merely acting on objects to obtain some goal. This involves novelty for its own sake, but the novel actions still develop by trial and error. Children do not know the outcome of their behavior until they try it.

To clarify the distinction between the stages of secondary and tertiary circular reactions, consider a child in his playpen with a variety of toys. A secondary circular reaction might involve the child dropping a block from shoulder height and watching it bounce off the floor. In repeating the action, the child would continue with the blocks and always release them from shoulder level. In the Tertiary Circular Reaction Stage, the child might vary the height of his release from his head to just barely above the floor. He might vary what he dropped, trying out all the toys available, or he might vary both the height and the toy simultaneously.*

The change from secondary to tertiary circular reactions can be illustrated with an episode from *The House at Pooh Corner* (Milne, 1961a). Pooh is walking in the forest holding a fir-cone when he trips, dropping the cone into the river.

> "That's funny," said Pooh. "I dropped it on the other side," said Pooh, "and it came out on this side! I wonder if it would do it again?" And he went back for some more fir-cones.
>
> It did. It kept on doing it. Then he dropped two in at once, and leant over the bridge to see which of them would come out first; and one of them did; but as they were both the same size, he didn't know if it was the one he wanted to win, or the other one. So the next time he dropped one big one and one little one. [P. 94]

The interesting event (the fir-cone floating under the bridge) happened literally by accident, and Pooh first attempted to

---

* Parents are urged to be patient if their child, playing this dropping game, happens to pitch the toys out of the playpen. After all, what are parents for, if not to retrieve the toys so that baby can drop them again? Parents should also not be surprised when peas and meat are dropped from the highchair. It is just a way of learning how these objects behave, although it is more likely that baby will learn how parents behave.

repeat it exactly, showing secondary circular reactions. Then he varied both the number and size of the cones, showing tertiary circular reactions.

STAGE 6: BEGINNING OF REPRESENTATIONAL THOUGHT

Stage 6 is the beginning of representational thought. Before this stage, children can solve problems and learn how to act deliberately and efficiently to achieve a desired goal. But Piaget stated that children do not start to *think without acting* before entering the sixth stage of the Sensorimotor Period. Representational thinking, according to Piaget, involves mentally reasoning about a problem *prior* to acting. Children try to solve problems using their familiar schemes, but if these fail, they will not grope around in the trial-and-error fashion of prior stages. Rather, now they will consider the situation mentally, perhaps drawing an analogy from a different time and place, and then directly act on the problem with a scheme never before applied to it. Piaget (1952) described his daughter's attempts to remove a chain from a matchbox which was not open enough for her to insert her hand and grasp the chain. According to Piaget's observations, many times before she had grasped the chain, but she had always been able to insert her hand through the opening. She first applied an old scheme, pushing her fingers into the box, but that did not work. In earlier stages of development, she might have applied other schemes such as shaking the box or biting it. Now Piaget observed her to open and close her mouth a little bit, then open it a bit wider and then still wider. Finally she put a finger into the opening of the matchbox, pulled it wider, and grasped the chain. Piaget believed she solved the problem by examining her old schemes mentally, rather than by trying each of them overtly. Reasoning by the analogy with opening her mouth wider, she invented a novel solution to her problem.

Piaget did not believe that the Sensorimotor child's thought involved language because the child's language development was still too rudimentary in this stage. As children first learn to speak, word meanings are unstable and idiosyncratic. Children do not realize that the meaning of a word must be agreed upon by the language community, so they change the meaning to suit their own purposes. For example, a child might use the syllable *mu* to represent first his milk, then a cookie, his dog, and finally his mother, all within the span of a few hours. By the end of the Sensorimotor Period, the child is using only one- or perhaps two-word utterances to label objects and express simple desires. Language usage is thus not developed enough to be useful for the new skill of representational thinking.

The six Sensorimotor stages span the child's development from the early reflexive behaviors to repetitions of various activities involving the child's own body and other objects to the beginning of mental reasoning prior to acting (see Table 2-2 for an outline of these stages). Children in the Sensorimotor Period use their behavioral schemes to manipulate objects, to learn some of the properties of objects, and to obtain goals by combining several schemes. Their behavior is tied to the concrete and the immediate, and they can only apply their schemes to objects they can perceive directly.

OBJECT PERMANENCE

The overview just presented of the Sensorimotor Period has focused on the inferred underlying structure of infancy, that is, on the various schemes an infant can use. An alternative way to view the period is to examine the development of a specific product of using the schemes: object permanence.

Object permanence is defined as the knowledge that objects continue to exist even when one is not perceiving them. You know that this book continues to exist even if you put it on a shelf and leave the room. If it is not there when you return,

TABLE 2-2

SIX STAGES OF THE SENSORIMOTOR PERIOD

Stage	Principal Characteristics
1. Modification of Reflexes (0–1 month)	Reflexes become efficient and more voluntary movements replace them
2. Primary Circular Reactions (1–4 months)	Repetition of interesting body movements
3. Secondary Circular Reactions (4–10 months)	Repetition of interesting external events
4. Coordination of Secondary Reactions (10–12 months)	Combining schemes to obtain a goal
5. Tertiary Circular Reactions (12–18 months)	Varying repetition for novelty
6. Beginning of Representational Thought (18–24 months)	Thinking prior to acting

you might start inquiring whether another person took it. Although the idea is sometimes appealing, you do not really believe that it could "vanish into thin air." Does the child have this same knowledge of the permanence of objects from birth, or is it something the child has to learn? Piaget suggested that object permanence is learned during the Sensorimotor Period in a series of stages defined by the infant's searching behaviors.* These six stages are shown in Table 2-3.

---

* The stages of object permanence development cut across the stages outlined above for the Sensorimotor Period. As a guide to the reader, approximate age ranges will be given in this discussion.

TABLE 2-3

SIX STAGES IN THE ACQUISITION
OF OBJECT PERMANENCE

Approximate Ages	Principal Characteristics
1. 0–2 months	No expectations or searching
2. 2–4 months	Passive expectations
3. 4–8 months	Search for partially covered objects
4. 8–12 months	Search for completely covered objects
5. 12–18 months	Search after visible displacements
6. 18+ months	Search after hidden displacements

According to Piaget, in the first stage (from birth to 2 months), children will look at objects in their visual field, but if the objects leave the visual field, the infants stop looking and change to some other activity. This results in the world being perceived as a series of fleeting images. Mother's face appears above the infant so he looks at her. If she steps away, he looks at something else. The next stage (from 2 to 4 months) is characterized by "passive expectations." For a short while infants will gaze at the location where an object disappeared, as if waiting for it to reappear. There is no active search, however, and Piaget does not credit the child with object permanence. He interprets the child's behavior as merely continuing an ongoing activity. Consider, for example, a girl waving a rattle. If the rattle accidentally slips from her hand to the floor, she will just continue waving her hand. She will not look around on the floor for the rattle.

In the next stage (roughly 4 to 8 months), children can anticipate the trajectory of an object and look for it at its landing place. This search is usually limited to looking for objects that children themselves have caused to disappear, but it shows what Piaget considered to be the beginnings of true object permanence. In this stage, children will also reach for a partially covered object. If it disappears completely, though, they will stop reaching.

From about 8 to 12 months, children will search for objects that other people have caused to disappear, but they cannot do so successfully (that is, find the object) if a series of movements (displacements) has to be considered. Piaget's demonstration of this involved showing a child a toy and then placing the toy under a cover. The child in this stage immediately lifts the cover and obtains the toy. This sequence is repeated, and again the child finds the toy. On the third trial, however, the child watches as the toy is hidden in a different location, under a pillow. Once it disappears from sight, the child turns away and looks for it under the cover where it was hidden the first two times. Although the child apparently knows that the object exists, he confers a certain "privilege of position" on it and includes in the definition of an object where it can be found.

By the beginning of the second year of life (12 to 18 months), children learn how to handle the displacements described above. They will search for the object where it was last seen. However, they have to see the displacements to be able to follow them. If the toy is hidden under the cover, the cover and the toy are both put under the pillow, and then only the cover is removed, children will not search for the toy under the pillow. Searching after hidden displacements occurs only after the final stage in the development of object permanence (18 months onward).

While Piaget's description of the child's active search for objects is accurate, one can ask whether active search is the best response to use as an indication of object permanence. A recurrent suspicion in developmental psychology is that because of lack of development in some related function, children may *know* something before they can demonstrate their knowledge. For example, children might know an object has permanence before they can actively search for it because active search involves the development of eye-hand coordination—to reach

33

where one is looking. Or children might know an object exists but forget about it due to a limited memory span. This latter hypothesis, in fact, was offered by Bower (1971) after he conducted an experiment on object permanence in young infants.

Bower's test of object permanence

Since Bower wanted to test very young infants, who would not reach for objects, he used a simple response, the surprise or startle reaction, as the potential indicator of object permanence. The babies in his experiment were either 20, 40, 80, or 100 days old, corresponding to infants in Piaget's first two stages in the development of object permanence. Bower propped each baby up in a sitting position so that the baby faced a brightly colored object, such as a ball. As the infant looked at the ball, a screen moved in front of it, hiding the ball from the infant's view. The screen remained in front of the ball for either 1½, 3, 7½, or 15 seconds. Then the screen moved away. On half of the trials, the ball was visible again. On the other half, the ball had disappeared. Bower reasoned that if the babies had a notion of object permanence, they should expect the ball to be visible again when the screen moved off. Its reappearance should produce no reaction, but if the ball had disappeared, the babies should be quite surprised. On the other hand, if infants have no notion of object permanence, they should be surprised to see the ball and not surprised if it had disappeared. In this experiment, surprise was measured by watching the babies' facial expressions. In other experiments, more sophisticated measures of heart rate and breathing changes have indicated the same results. Figure 2-1 presents the alternative outcomes possible.

The results of this little experiment depended upon the age of the baby and the length of time the screen hid the ball. All age groups of babies were surprised when the ball was gone if the screen had been hiding it for only 1½ seconds. None were surprised on the trials when the ball was still there. To-

34

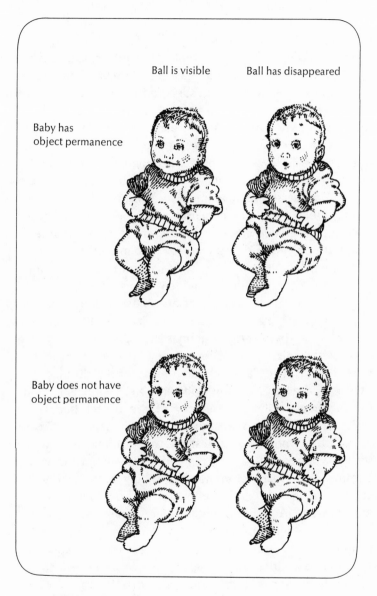

Ball is visible   Ball has disappeared

Baby has
object permanence

Baby does not have
object permanence

Figure 2-1. Possible reactions by babies with or without object permanence, depending on the conditions of the experiment

gether these two results indicated some object permanence by infants as young as 20 days. The oldest infants expected the ball to be there even after the longest time interval. The youngest infants, however, were more surprised to see the ball remain than disappear at the longest time interval. That is, after 15 seconds of hiding, the youngest babies appeared not to have object permanence (see Figure 2-2). Apparently, then, 20-day-old babies will show some object permanence if the conditions are proper (only 1½ seconds of hiding), but lack of development in processes such as memory prevents the infant from having a fully developed conception of object permanence.

Piaget disagreed with Bower's interpretation of these results, saying it "only serves to prove that recognition is a very early phenomenon and in no way does it confirm the permanency . . . of the object while it is hidden" (Piaget & Inhelder, 1976, p. 32). By repeatedly looking at an object, children can form a static copy or image of it and recognize it in a limited sense, but the concept of object permanence can only come from children organizing the schemes they have used on that and other objects. For Piaget, children must form a distinction between themselves as actors and the objects they act upon to fully appreciate the permanency of the object (see Gratch, 1975, for a detailed contrast of the views of Piaget and Bower).

The object permanence test described above used a static scene. What would happen if the object was moving when it became hidden, for example, if a rolling ball went under a couch? Or what if a ball went under the couch but a doll came out? Bower (1971) performed another experiment which addressed this question, although his original purpose was to investigate which features of an object (size, shape, color, speed) help an infant to recognize that an object which reappeared is the same as the one which disappeared. Bower argued that if a ball disappeared but a doll reappeared and the infant looked around for the ball, then object permanence would be indicated.

The infants who served as subjects in this experiment were

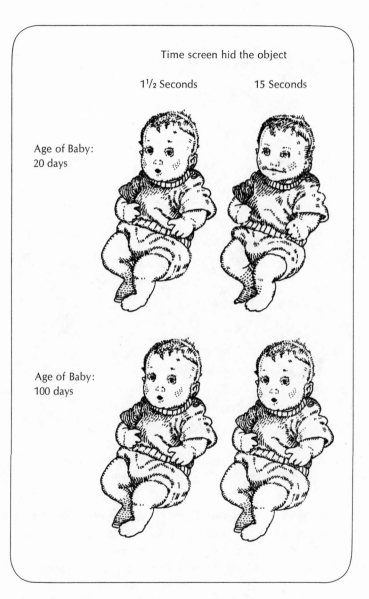

Time screen hid the object

1½ Seconds   15 Seconds

Age of Baby:
20 days

Age of Baby:
100 days

Figure 2-2. Surprise and nonsurprise reactions obtained on trials when the ball has disappeared in Bower's experiment on object permanence

Figure 2-3. Location of baby, screen, and railroad track
in Bower's experiment on object recognition

between 6 and 22 weeks of age. Each infant was seated facing
a screen, and a railroad track ran from left to right, passing behind the screen (see Figure 2-3). Each baby was exposed to
four different situations. In the first situation, a small white
mannikin was placed at the left end of the track. It then moved
along the track at a constant speed, passed behind the screen,
and emerged from the other side, stopping at the right end of
the track. After a short pause, the mannikin reversed directions,
moving back to the original left end of the track, again passing

38

behind the screen. All babies followed the movement with their eyes, tracking the mannikin.

In the second condition, the white mannikin moved along the track, and at the time when it should have reappeared from behind the screen, an entirely different object, a red lion, emerged. The red lion traveled to the right end of the track, paused, moved back behind the screen, and the white mannikin reappeared, moving to the left end of the track. Seeing a difference in size, shape, and color, adults would conclude that two objects were being used. Babies over 16 weeks old followed the motion of the lion when it emerged, but some of them glanced back at the screen. When the lion paused at the right end of the track, there were definite looks back at the screen about one quarter of the time. This was taken as an indication that many of the babies knew that two objects had been involved. Babies under 16 weeks of age showed a very different pattern of responses. They tracked the moving object with no glancing back toward the screen. If the mannikin is not a permanent object, then of course a lion can emerge.

In the third condition, the white mannikin moved toward the right and went behind the screen. According to its speed of movement, the mannikin should have been behind the screen for a certain length of time. In this condition, a white mannikin emerged "too fast." That is, just after the first white mannikin disappeared behind the screen, an identical one emerged from the far side of the screen. As in the other two conditions, the entire sequence was repeated in reverse. Adults will take this as an indication of two different but identical-looking objects. All the babies over 16 weeks of age looked back at the screen after the one object had stopped, apparently waiting for the second one to emerge. Babies under 16 weeks of age got very upset and refused to look anymore. They did not track the movement of the object that emerged.

The fourth condition was a combination of the previous two. As the white mannikin moved toward the right and passed behind the screen, a red lion emerged "too fast." The reactions

39

to this condition resembled responses to the third condition. Babies over 16 weeks looked back at the screen after they had tracked the emerging object. Babies under 16 weeks cried and refused to look. Table 2-4 summarizes these results.

Bower's results suggest two conclusions. First, before 16 weeks, infants do not use information about size, shape, and color to make decisions about the *identity* of objects. They use speed of movement instead. Although they can *perceive* size, shape, and color differences (see Chapter 3), they do not use these features in identifying objects. Older infants, in contrast, use all the features to identify an object. Second, by 16 weeks, some infants visually searched for the mannikin by glancing back at the screen when the lion emerged. If active looking is an active search, then this evidence cannot be dismissed as mere "passive expectations." Thus Bower's results could indicate object permanence one or two months earlier than Piaget found. Why hiding a moving object should produce active searching earlier than covering a stationary object is not yet known. As we will see in other sections of this chapter, the particular task selected to demonstrate some cognitive competency affects the age at which the skill seems to emerge.

Despite disagreements about how early one can find signs of object permanence, the sequence of stages which Piaget documented have been reaffirmed in other research. In fact, the same first four stages have also been found in cats (Gruber, Girgus, & Banuazizi, 1971), and all six stages have been found in rhesus monkeys (Wise, Wise, & Zimmermann, 1974). The value of Piaget's contribution lies in the discovery that the child's concept of object permanence undergoes significant changes during the Sensorimotor Period.

It is no coincidence that the last object permanence stage, searching after a hidden displacement, occurs during the last stage of the Sensorimotor Period. To follow a hidden displacement, a child must be able to form a mental representation of the missing object and to anticipate mentally the results of moving the first cover behind the second. The emergence and

TABLE 2-4

RESULTS OF BOWER'S EXPERIMENT ON OBJECT RECOGNITION

Objects	Speed	Age of Babies	
		Under 16 weeks	Over 16 weeks
Cond. 1. Mannikin	Normal	Track moving object	Track moving object
Cond. 2. Mannikin→Lion	Normal	Track moving object	Track moving object and some glances at screen
Cond. 3. Mannikin	Too fast	Refuse to look	Track moving object and look back at screen
Cond. 4. Mannikin→Lion	Too fast	Refuse to look	Track moving object and look back at screen

use of mental representations marks the final development in the Sensorimotor Period and sets the stage for the second major period of cognitive development, the Preoperational Period.

THE PREOPERATIONAL PERIOD

The distinguishing characteristic of the Preoperational child is the development of *symbolic functions.** Symbolic functioning is the ability to make one thing represent a different thing which is not present. The degree of correspondence between the symbol and its referent can vary from highly concrete to highly abstract. That is, if one uses a toy hammer made of plastic to represent a real metal hammer, the degree of correspondence is highly concrete. A mental picture or image of a hammer is more abstract but may retain some features of the thing represented, such as color and shape. The word made up of the letters *h, a, m, m, e, r* is a highly abstract symbol for the real object since printed letters on a page bear an arbitrary relationship to the metal tool. Piaget argued that the acquisition of symbolic functions enables children to increase their sphere of activity to include past and future events as well as present ones. That is, they can apply their schemes to nonimmediate events. This use of symbolic functions is one of the major distinctions between children in the Preoperational Period and those in the Sensorimotor Period.

SYMBOLIC FUNCTIONS

Symbolic functions have been inferred from four types of activities seen in Preoperational children: search for hidden objects, delayed imitation, symbolic play, and language. Having acquired object permanence, as discussed earlier, Preopera-

---

* These have also been called *semiotic functions* (Piaget & Inhelder, 1976).

42

tional children can follow hidden displacements. In order to guide their searching behavior, children must have some sort of mental representation of the hidden object and of the unseen movements of displacement. At younger ages when children would only search if they perceived the object, the perception of the object could be said to guide the search. Now some kind of symbolic function must take over the guidance.

Delayed imitation is, as the name implies, imitation of a behavior some time after it was observed. It is postulated that as children observe a model, they form an internal representation of the modeled behavior. Later the recall of this internal representation controls imitation. Piaget rejected the idea that language was the primary mode of internal representation used in delayed imitation and search for hidden objects because the behaviors displayed are much too complex for the child to describe verbally. He cited the example of his daughter who one day watched a playmate throw a temper tantrum, stamping his feet and howling (Piaget, 1951). The next day Piaget's daughter stood up in her playpen, stamped her feet, and howled just as she had seen the friend do the day before. Her actions had a deliberateness about them which suggested that she was trying out a new behavior, to see what it was like. Without a symbolic means of learning and then recalling the temper tantrum actions, his daughter could not have imitated them a day later.

In symbolic play, the child treats an object as if it were something else. This is readily seen in a child's use of a broomstick as a plane, a doll as a friend, or fingers as guns. One object is made to stand for another in the make-believe world of play.

In the Preoperational Period, language begins to be used symbolically, as children describe activities of the past and understand some references to the future. Their use of words is more conventional, though by no means perfectly adultlike. While the meaning of a word is now stable, the name of an object is seen as such an integral part of the object that changing the name changes the object. Recall the examples in Chapter 1 when Susan thought that renaming her would make her a boy and calling the sun the moon would produce darkness during the day. Besides giving children an efficient way to communicate with others, language has two other uses: it helps children control their own behavior, and it teaches them how to classify and organize their environment. The behavioral-control use is quite striking when children tell themselves what to do or not do. For example, a child can be seen approaching a forbidden object like a hot stove and saying out loud, "No, don't touch," just before withdrawing his outstretched hand. (Even some adults have been known to talk out loud to aid their concentration during problem solving.) The classification use of language enables children to group objects together because of shared labels. For instance, children can guess that a beanbag chair is good for sitting on, even though it does not have four legs, because it has been called a chair. Similarly, any strange offering called "candy" will probably taste good. Preoperational children thus begin to learn about the formal properties of classes.

PROPERTIES OF CLASSES

Classes are, in essence, the categories into which we divide objects. These class divisions can be made along one or more dimensions (or properties) of the objects. For example, one can classify objects according to their shapes, resulting in the classes of square objects, circular objects, and triangular objects. Alternatively, one can classify objects according to their color, resulting in the classes of red things, blue things, green things, and yellow things. One of the properties of classes is that no object may belong to two classes *along the same dimension* simultaneously. Thus a large blue square could, if classified according to shape, belong to the class of square things, but it could not simultaneously belong to a class of circular things or triangular things. It could, however, also belong to another class based on a different dimension such as color. In other words, classes along one dimension are mutually exclusive, but classes along independent dimensions may overlap.

All objects in one class have some common trait. A large blue square and a small red square share squareness. This property, squareness, gives the class its definition and is called its *intension*. Circularity is the intension of a class of circles. Blueness is the intension, the defining characteristic, of the class of blue objects.

A class can also be described by listing its members. This is the *extension* of the class. The extension of a class of flowers could be roses, tulips, pansies, and daisies. Finally, the intension of a class determines its extension. If the intension of a class is "fully enclosed, stationary structures in which people live," the extension of the class must include tents, teepees, houses, cottages, and hotels.

MULTIPLE CLASSIFICATION

During the Preoperational Period, children come to know some of the basic properties of classes. They demonstrate this knowledge by sorting objects according to various classes. One typical task, called the multiple classification problem, is to present children with an array of cards such as pink and yellow, large and small, circles and squares. Children with a firm understanding of class properties can sort the cards into two groups in three separate ways, according to each of the three dimensions, color, size, and shape. Children who do not yet have a full understanding of classes will show any of several common mistakes. The first mistake to appear is not sorting the cards at all. Children might not know what is being asked of them, they might think the task is too difficult, or they simply might not want to cooperate. Frosty the Snowman was the product of one child asked to sort cards (see Figure 2-4a). The second error to

Figure 2-4. Typical sorting errors on a multiple classification task

a. "Frosty the Snowman" was created by a child who ignored the instructions to sort the cards into two piles.
b. This arrangement was created by a child who changed dimensions from pink to square for one of the two piles.
c. This arrangement was created by a child who formed discrete piles of identical objects.

appear is to change the basis of the groupings several times. One boy started out putting all pink things together. He placed two pink circles next to each other, then a pink small square, and then changed the dimension of the sort to shape and put a large yellow square next, followed by a small yellow square (see Figure 2-4b). No single intension, or defining property, regulated his sorting. The third mistake is to sort according to all dimensions simultaneously, ignoring the instructions to form only two piles. One girl formed discrete groups of small yellow circles, small pink circles, large yellow squares, and so forth. Classes for this girl consisted only of identical objects rather than of objects sharing a trait (see Figure 2-4c).

By the end of the Preoperational Period, children demonstrate a basic understanding of classes. When asked to sort cards, they will choose one dimension (e.g., size) to serve as the basis for the sort. All objects having a certain value along the dimension (e.g., the intension, large) will be placed together, while those objects having another value along the same dimension (e.g., the intension, small) will be amassed. Moreover, no objects will be left out of the sort.

Thus we have seen that Preoperational children are more advanced than Sensorimotor children because Preoperational children have mental representations as well as behavioral schemes. These mental representations are inferred from various tasks (search for hidden objects, delayed imitation, make-believe play, and language) which all exemplify symbolic functions. In addition, children in the Preoperational Period show some understanding of classes. Despite these accomplishments, the thinking of Preoperational children is, as the name implies, still not "operational." Preoperational children have mental representations, but Piaget did not believe that their thinking met the second defining characteristic of operations, being "reversible." In addition, Piaget asserted that Preoperational children are unable to focus their attention on different dimensions of a problem simultaneously. For example, the matrix problem shown in Figure 2-5 is a basic classification task extended to two dimensions simultaneously. Preoperational children fail to consider both number and shape and so would find the four-triangle card as acceptable as the three-triangle one, or would find the three-X card as acceptable as the three-triangle one.

47

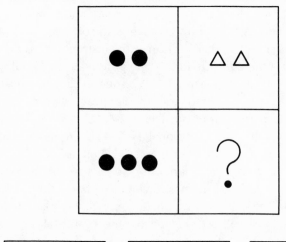

  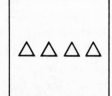

Figure 2-5. A two-dimension matrix problem. Children select one of the three lower cards to replace the question
mark.

Piaget called this focusing of attention *centration* when
decentration is required to reach the solution. Centration
shows up in three tasks which Preoperational children fail but
Concrete Operational children pass: seriation, class inclusion,
and conservation.

SERIATION

The seriation problem asks children to put elements in a series
according to one quantifiable dimension. That is, the task is to
arrange objects in some order relative to each other. For ex-

48

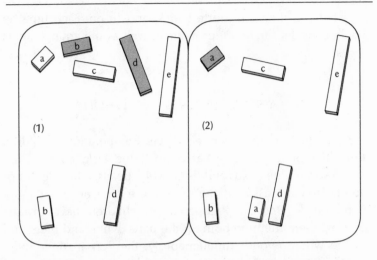

Figure 2-6. Typical error in sorting sticks according to their lengths

1. Two sticks (b and d) are randomly selected from the pile and compared. The shorter is placed to the left.
2. One of the remaining sticks (a) is randomly selected from the pile, compared to one of the previously sorted sticks (d), and placed to the left of (d) since it is shorter. No comparison is made between sticks (a) and (b).

ample, children are given a series of sticks of differing lengths and told to arrange them from shortest to longest. A Preoperational child might proceed as follows: he would take two sticks from the main pile, compare them, and put the shorter of the two on the left. Then he would take another stick from the pile and compare it with only one of the two prior sticks. If it was shorter, he would place it to the left without regard for its length relative to the other original stick (see Figure 2-6). Piaget's explanation for the Preoperational child's behavior is that he can focus on only one aspect of the problem at a time. In the previous example, the child focused on one paired comparison at a time rather than on the total array. An older child might solve the seriation problem by scanning the main pile, removing the shortest stick, scanning the pile again and removing what was then the shortest stick, and so on. Each time he would consider the entire problem as well as the arrangements he was forming.

CLASS INCLUSION (PART—WHOLE)

The class inclusion problem also gives Preoperational children difficulties. In a common variation of the task, children are shown seven blue beads and three white beads, all made out of wood. They are asked if there are more blue beads or more wood beads. Because Preoperational children have trouble focusing their attention both on the parts (white and blue) and on the whole (wood) simultaneously, they err in their judgments. The following is an interchange between a five-year-old boy and an adult.

Adult: Do you see all these beads I have? Some of them are blue and some are white. What do you think the blue beads are made of?
Child: Wood.
Adult: That's right. And what do you think the white ones are made of?
Child: Wood.
Adult: Good. Both the blue beads and the white beads are made of wood. Now I have a question for you. Do you think there are more blue beads or wood beads?
Child: Blue.
Adult: Why?
Child: Because there are more.
Adult: More what?
Child: More blue.
Adult: More blue than what?
Child: More blue than white.
Thinking that the child might have misheard the question, the adult attempted more directive questions.

Adult: But I wanted to know about the wooden beads. Are the white beads made out of wood?
Child: Yes.
Adult: Are the blue beads made out of wood?
Child: Yes.
Adult: So all the beads are made of wood?
Child: Yes.
Adult: So are there more *wood* beads or blue beads?
Child: Blue.

This child was not really being stubborn. He was just unable to make the necessary comparison across the two levels of the hierarchy, that is, across the two subordinate classes based on color (blue and white) and the superordinate class based on material (wood). Piaget maintained that children would have to focus on the two levels of classes at the same time in order to solve the class inclusion problem. Such an ability is characteristic of children in the next major period of development, the Concrete Operational Period.

CONSERVATION

In addition to their difficulty with the class inclusion and seriation problems, Preoperational children do not succeed in conservation tasks. In any of the various conservation tasks, children watch the tester change some features of a display and must decide that some other feature does not change. For example, if two quantities are equal along one dimension, such as number, but appear to be unequal along another dimension, such as length or density, Preoperational children will be mistaken in their judgments concerning numerical equality. The task can be presented as follows: on a table between the child and the tester, a row of five red checkers is placed. Below the five red checkers are placed five black ones, aligned so that each black checker is directly below a red one (see Figure 2-7a).

51

Figure 2-7. A conservation of number task with checkers

a. The starting arrangement from the child's point of view.
b. The experimenter spreads out one row.
c. The ending arrangement from the child's point of view.

The child is asked if the two rows have the same number of checkers, if the red row has more, or if the black row has more. Children above about the age of three will say that the rows have the same number. As the child watches, the black row is spread out (see Figure 2-7b) until the arrangement seen in Figure 2-7c is created. Then the child is again asked if the two rows have the same number of checkers or if one row has more than the other. Preoperational children reply either that the black row has more "because it is longer" or that the red row has more "because they are all bunched up" (more dense). In contrast, children in the Concrete Operational Period will correctly reply that the numbers have stayed the same, recognizing that perceptual changes in length or density have no effect on numerical quantity.

Piaget found that Concrete Operational children tend to offer three types of reasons for their conservation responses. The *counting* justification proves the two rows equal by counting each row. A *one-to-one correspondence* response reflects the idea that for every checker in the red row, there is a corresponding checker in the black row. In the *associativity* response, children state that rearranging the parts does not affect the whole. To put it in the words of an eight-year-old, "All you did was spreaded them out."

To make sure that the idea of conservation of number had generality and was not restricted to rows of checkers, Piaget devised several different conservation of number tasks. In one of them, children are given a pile of ten cars and shown two jars. One jar is tall and thin; the other is short and wide. Children are instructed to take a car in each hand and drop each car in the jar in front of their hands at the same time. After they do this five times, of course, there are five cars in each jar, but the tall thin jar appears to be full while the short wide one is not (see Figure 2-8). Children are then asked if each jar has the same number of cars. Preoperational children who do not conserve number either point to the tall thin jar as having more,

Figure 2-8. A conservation of number task with cars

a. The starting arrangement.
b. The child places a car in each container simultaneously.
c. The ending arrangement.

because it is taller or because it is "all filled up," or they point to the short wide jar, saying it has more because it is "fatter."

In summary, we have seen that Preoperational children use symbolic functions and begin to understand classes, but they fail to compare parts to wholes (in the class inclusion problem), do not order serial quantities well (seriation problem), and do not conserve number. Piaget attributed these limitations in thinking to Preoperational children's inability to decenter their attention and to their lack of true operations.

THE CONCRETE OPERATIONAL PERIOD

In contrast to Preoperational children, Concrete Operational children can solve a variety of tasks. When asked whether there are more blue beads or wood beads, Concrete Operational children can state that the wood beads are a larger class. They can place sticks in a series by length, and they can conserve number.

OPERATIONS

Why do Concrete Operational children succeed when Preoperational children fail? Piaget proposed that Concrete Operational children have new structures, called *operations,* which permit them to transform a mental "action" (i.e., a thought). These transformations can reverse the effect of the original action, compensate for it, or leave it unchanged. *Reversibility by inversion,* for example, involves applying two operations successively such that the original identity is regained. Addition and subtraction are inverse operations. Say that the original state is one item. After adding two to obtain three, we can subtract two and return to the original one.

Reversibility by compensation also involves applying two operations in succession, but this time an equivalent state, rather than the original state, is obtained. Cowan (1978) explained this reversibility with an example about the area of a rectangle. Say that the original area is the length, L, multiplied by the width, W. If the length were doubled, to 2L, and the width were halved, to $\frac{1}{2}$W, the area of the new rectangle, 2L $\times$ $\frac{1}{2}$W, would be equivalent to the first rectangle, L $\times$ W, but the two rectangles would not be identical in shape. Doubling and halving are compensating operations.

A third operation, called *identity*, can leave a state unchanged. Adding zero, for example, is an identity operation because the quantity does not change even though a mental action has been taken.

Piaget suggested that Concrete Operational children can solve conservation tasks because of these operations. Consider again the conservation of number task with rows of checkers. A Concrete Operational child might focus on the tester's action of spreading out one row. The child can mentally picture the opposite action, compressing the row, to get back to the original length and therefore conclude that the number of checkers has not changed. A child using this inversion operation might justify his conservation response by saying, "All you did was spread them out and you could put them back together again." It is also possible to solve the conservation problem using the compensation operation. Concrete Operational children see that one row has increased in length but decreased in density. Since length and density are reciprocal features, a change in one compensates for a change in the other, resulting in no net change for the display. Using the identity operation, Concrete Operational children see that nothing (zero) has been added or subtracted, so number has not changed. In the Preoperational Period, children tend to focus on the beginning state (the apparent equality of the two rows) and the end state (with its perceptual inequality in length) and ignore the intervening activity, or they focus on the initial action (spreading out) but cannot reverse their thinking to consider the potential inverse compressing action.

Conservation tasks

As with each new cognitive skill children acquire, it takes practice to apply that skill correctly and efficiently to new problems. Concrete Operational children, having mastered conservation of number, must also master conservation of other dimensions such as liquid quantity, mass, and length. The liquid quantity conservation task is very similar to the conservation of number task. Children are shown two identical beakers filled with identical amounts of colored water. They first judge the beakers to have equal amounts. Then, as they watch, the liquid is poured from one of the original beakers into a taller, thinner beaker. The children are next asked to compare the newly filled beaker with the other original one (see Figure 2-9a). An alternative form of the liquid quantity task involves pouring the liquid from one beaker into five smaller containers. The nonconserving child will either indicate that the original beaker has more because it is taller or that the five smaller containers have more because there are five of them. The classical problem for conservation of mass presents children with two identical clay balls. Then one is either rolled into a sausage or flattened like a pancake (see Figure 2-9b). To conserve, children must recognize that changes in shape do not indicate changes in mass. In the conservation of length task, children must judge that length stays the same even though position has shifted (see Figure 2-9c). In all, approximately ten different conservation tasks test for the recognition of preservation of equality in the face of compelling changes in spatial arrangement.

Although Piaget did not suggest that children ought to conserve colors, Milne (1961b) captured the spirit of the conservation problem in an episode from *Winnie-the-Pooh*. Piglet had a large red balloon, "one of those big coloured things you blow up," to give to Eeyore as a birthday present. On the way, he fell, and it burst.

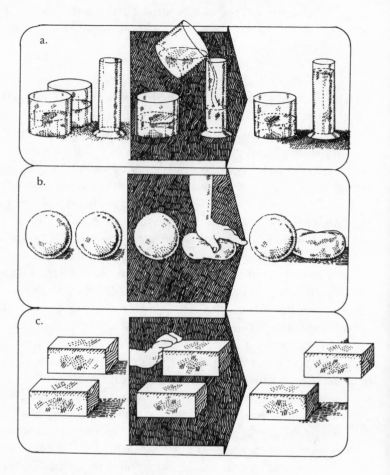

Figure 2-9. Tasks testing for conservation of liquid, mass, and length

a. Conservation of liquid.
b. Conservation of mass.
c. Conservation of length.

There was a very long silence.
"My balloon?" said Eeyore at last.
Piglet nodded.
"My birthday balloon?"
"Yes, Eeyore," said Piglet sniffling a little. "Here it is. With—with many happy returns of the day." And he gave Eeyore the small piece of damp rag.
"Is this it?" said Eeyore, a little surprised.
Piglet nodded.
"My present?"
Piglet nodded again.
"The balloon?"
"Yes."
"Thank you, Piglet," said Eeyore. "You don't mind my asking," he went on, "but what colour was this balloon when it—when it *was* a balloon?" [Pp. 86-87]

RESEARCH ISSUES

As we did for the Sensorimotor Period, we have presented the supposed underlying structures (symbolic functions and operations) and specific abilities (e.g., language and conservation) of the Preoperational and Concrete Operational periods. Piaget's descriptions and explanations of the Preoperational and Concrete Operational periods have provoked considerable research, only a small portion of which can be presented here. The first wave of research was aimed primarily at confirming (or disconfirming) Piaget's descriptions of the various stages and periods of development. It is probable that so much energy was spent in replicative research because Piaget's early methodology appeared weak in contrast to traditional American research. In brief, Piaget's approach was a flexible questioning procedure, permitting the tester to rephrase questions that the child did not understand and encouraging the child to expand brief verbal responses. The latter in particular is a delicate procedure because the tester must be careful not to suggest answers to the child. At the same time, the tester wants to be sure that the child offers his full thoughts and best reasons. Piaget was well aware of this problem, but he gave no indication of controlling for it experimentally. Also, in the books which first were translated into English, it appeared that Piaget based his conclusions on small samples of children and rarely subjected his results to statistical analysis.* One would have thought that a red flag had been waved in the face of a scientific bull. Moreover, Piaget's report of the Preoperational child's failure to solve conservation, seriation, and class inclusion problems was quite startling. This alone would have warranted replication research.

The evidence from the replicative studies is quite impressive. The response patterns Piaget noted for Genevan children were also found for other European, North and South American, African, and Asian children (Dasen, 1977). Testing with deaf, blind, and retarded children revealed the same developmental sequences as for normal children, although the rates of development are often slower for the handicapped, and the retarded may never progress very far through the stages (Brekke, Williams, & Tait, 1974; Gruen & Vore, 1972; Millar, 1976; Youniss, 1974).

Researchers then turned to other questions. One recurring question is: Do Preoperational children fail a task because they lack operations, as Piaget maintained, or because the task requires other skills or knowledge which Preoperational children lack? Note that this is the same type of question asked about Sensorimotor children's performance on the object permanence task. Can Preoperational children pass the various Concrete Operational tasks at an earlier age than Piaget suggested if changes are made in the specific task or if training is provided to make up for the specific skill deficit? The answer is clearly "yes."

---

* Piaget's later works rely less on children's verbal explanations, are based on larger samples, and contain comparisons between experimental and control groups when necessary.

Class inclusion studies

Gelman (1978) has reviewed the research on the class inclusion problem and has concluded that at least six factors can influence preschool children's success on it. We shall examine one factor to illustrate the general form of the argument. When we construct categories or groups of related objects, a classification can be made by *classes* or by *collections*. Membership in a class can be determined by matching an object's properties to the intension of the class. If the superordinate class of wood beads is defined by "round wooden objects with one centered hole" and a subordinate class member (a specific blue wood bead) fits that definition, then the subordinate object is also a member of the superordinate class. Inspection of the one object is sufficient to determine its membership in the class. Piaget described the stimulus materials in his class inclusion task with class nouns. To define a collection, however, the relationship between objects is important. A forest, for instance, is a collection of trees. Inspection of a single tree's attributes is not sufficient for deciding that the tree is a member of the forest. Similarly, a family is a (superordinate) collection composed of the subordinate classes parents and children. Children alone are not a family.

In a comparison of the two types of categories, the class inclusion test can be given using exactly the same stimulus materials but describing them either with class nouns or collection nouns. For example, children can be shown six oak trees and two pine trees and asked to compare the number of pine trees to all the trees (class noun) or the number of pine trees to the number of trees in the forest (collection noun). Or the children can be shown red and blue blocks and asked to compare the blue blocks to the blocks (class noun) or the blue blocks to the pile of blocks (collection noun). Kindergarten and first grade children who fail Piaget's standard class inclusion test succeed when collections are used (Markman & Siebert, 1976; Trabasso, Isen, Dolecki, McLanahan, Riley, & Tucker, 1978). "The major factor promoting successful performance seems to be unambiguous reference to the class as a whole and avoidance of procedures stressing distinctive features of the subordinate class" (Trabasso et al., 1978, p. 177). Piaget's original task with true classes seems to demand a higher degree of sophistication or knowledge than the modified versions of the task. The conclusion to be drawn is that Preoperational children can make subordinate-superordinate comparisons in some cases (with collections) before other cases (with true classes).

Conservation studies

For the conservation problem, researchers have followed the same strategy. Variations in the task have been tried, such as changing the specific stimulus materials, the words used in the questions to the children, and the children's responses (e.g., they can be asked merely to judge the stimuli as the same or different or to give a verbal explanation of their judgment). The bulk of the research, however, has used a training paradigm to see if children fail conservation tests because they are deficient in a particular skill unrelated to operations. The logic of using training studies is that some skill or knowledge, absent in nonconserving children, is provided by training. If after training children now pass the conservation tests, then one might conclude that Piaget's original tests were unnecessarily difficult or confusing. Just such a proposal was offered by Gelman (1969).

She hypothesized that young children might conserve if their attention were not so attracted to highly salient but irrelevant perceptual cues such as height, width, size, shape, and color. In the conservation of liquid quantity task, children are faced with two identical beakers containing equal amounts of water. From the child's point of view, quantity is a multidimensional concept, and decisions might be reached on the basis of any one of several salient dimensions: height, width, or shape of the beaker, water level, or actual amount. From the experimenter's point of view, only the last, actual amount, is a relevant dimension. Often equality of amount coincides with equality on the other dimensions, so the child must learn which of the dimensions to attend to. Furthermore, when the liquid is poured into the new beaker, all of the dimensions *except* actual amount are changed. It is well known that changing a dimension is one way to attract attention to it. It is likely, therefore, that younger children will attend to one of the irrelevant dimensions. If their attention is misdirected, then that will mask any attempts to find out whether they have logical operations such as addition, subtraction, or compensation.

Gelman trained children to attend and respond to actual amount and to ignore the other, irrelevant information. The subjects were children in kindergarten, about five years old. These children were chosen because they had failed to conserve on each of four conservation tasks (mass, liquid quantity, number, and length) in a pretest (a test before training). Figure 2-10 shows the tasks used in the pretest.

Training took place on two consecutive days, with eight sets of problems on length and eight sets on number each day. In each training trial, the child was confronted with three stimuli, two of which were identical and one which was different. For example, two sticks might be 6 inches long and one 10 inches. On half the trials, the child was asked to point to two things that were the same; on the other half, he was asked to point to two things that were different. The trials were arranged so as to reduce progressively the number of irrelevant cues which the child could use to make a correct response. On the first trial of a set, all cues indicated the correct response. For example, in the length problem, the two identical sticks would be placed horizontally, in parallel, with ends aligned, while the third stick might be slightly vertical with neither end aligned to the other two sticks. On trials 2-5, various placements of the sticks would make the child choose incorrectly if he used some of the irrelevant cues. On the sixth trial, none

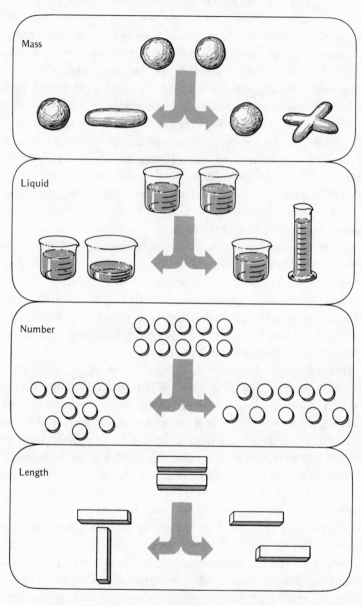

Figure 2-10. Conservation tasks used for the pretest in Gelman's experiment

of the irrelevant cues suggested a correct response. For example, the three sticks would be spatially separated, nonparallel, with no ends aligned. If the child answered correctly, it could only be on the basis of the relevant cue, actual length.* Figure 2-11 gives an example of the six trials per set for a length task.

Two groups of children, trained individually, received identical experiences with the training stimuli with one exception: whether or not they received feedback. In the experimental group, if subjects chose correctly, they were told they were correct and were given a small trinket; if they chose incorrectly, they were told they were wrong, and the next problem was presented. Subjects in the control group did not receive feedback after a trial. At the end of each session, they were told that they had played well.

All children were given two more conservation tests, one test on the day following training (the immediate posttest) and one test two to three weeks later (the delayed posttest). These posttests were comparable to the pretest and did not involve feedback. Table 2-5 shows the percentages of correct responses by the two groups of children for the four conservation tasks. On the length and number tasks, for which there had been explicit training, the experimental group got nearly perfect scores, whereas the control group got only one-quarter to one-third correct. Thus, conservation can be taught to children earlier than it typically occurs. Gelman's study also clearly showed that the experimental group improved on other conservation tasks as well (mass and liquid), even though these had not been trained.

Gelman concluded that two factors were important for training. First, children need an opportunity to work with many different arrangements of materials. This is what the control group did, and some specific learning did occur. The second important factor is feedback which indicates to the children which definition of quantity they should use. In other words,

---

* This same procedure, called *fading,* can be used to teach many different kinds of discriminations between stimuli.

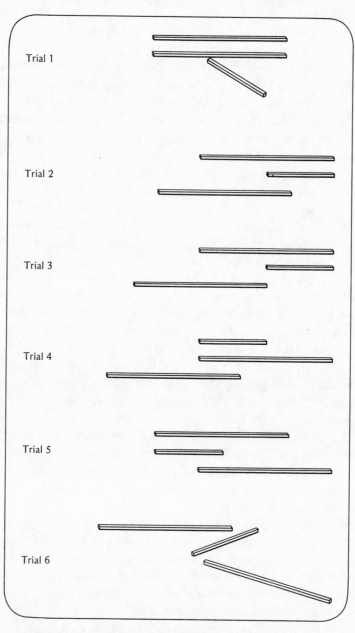

Trial 1

Trial 2

Trial 3

Trial 4

Trial 5

Trial 6

Figure 2-11. Examples of six trials for training conservation of length in Gelman's experiment

66

TABLE 2-5

AVERAGE PERCENTAGE OF CORRECT RESPONSES IN GELMAN'S EXPERIMENT

| | Immediate Posttest | | | |
	Length	Number	Mass	Liquid
Feedback during Training (Experimental Group)	95%	96%	58%	55%
No Feedback during Training (Control Group)	27%	21%	9%	4%

| | Delayed Posttest | | | |
	Length	Number	Mass	Liquid
Feedback during Training (Experimental Group)	90%	96%	65%	71%
No Feedback during Training (Control Group)	31%	29%	14%	3%

they need information about which dimension is relevant. With both feedback and opportunity, the experimental group learned a considerable amount about conservation tasks which were like the tasks on which they had trained (length and number), and they transferred this knowledge to two other conservation tasks (mass and liquid quantity).

Gelman's experiment demonstrated that some children do not give correct conservation responses because their attention is drawn to irrelevant aspects of the task. As soon as their attention is redirected, through training, they quickly solve the conservation problems. Does this mean that the children already had mental operations? That question cannot be answered because mental operations are not directly observable; like any hypothetical construct, they can only be inferred from performance. Was an attentional deficit the only factor impeding the expression of conservation? Probably not, because many other kinds of training studies have been successful, including teaching a generalized rule to express the conservation principle, providing an opportunity to watch peer models who conserve, and staging debates between conserving and nonconserving peers (see Brainerd, 1977, and Brainerd & Allen, 1971, for reviews of the training literature). The training results suggest that many different factors play a role in the development of conservation in children and/or that children can achieve an understanding of conservation by a variety of paths.

It is not particularly damaging to Piaget's theory to have children develop conservation earlier than he noted, as long as the sequence of development remains constant. Piaget's writings do mention typical ages when he observed the various conservation and classification tasks to be solved. Only those who misinterpret Piaget's position to be strictly maturational would insist that hard-and-fast age ranges should be established. Piaget himself did not take that position. He was interested in describing the sequences and processes of cognitive development, not in establishing norms of development or in rank-ordering children as the intelligence-testing movement has done. It was the characteristic errors children made that guided Piaget's research. Age was of secondary importance, serving only as a general guideline to the probable level of development of a child.

As Beilin (1981) remarked, it is ironic that critics of Piaget fault him for underestimating young children's knowledge when he was responsible for focusing researchers' attention on the cognitive accomplishments (and deficits) of young children. Those accomplishments in the Concrete Operational Period, in solving conservation, seriation, and class inclusion problems, are outstanding in comparison to Preoperational children's skills. Nevertheless, Concrete Operational children are limited to applying their mental operations to problems which they have personally experienced or which have some physical manifestation (such as sticks to move or liquid to pour). They do not readily solve purely verbal, abstract, hypothetical problems, and they tend to reject hypotheses which violate known facts. For example, one can ask the following question: If all dogs were green, and I had a dog, would it be green too? Concrete Operational children will balk at such a question, rejecting the initial supposition by stating that dogs cannot be green. Formal Operational children, in the last major period of cognitive development, are more likely to solve the problem.

THE FORMAL OPERATIONAL PERIOD

Children (or adolescents) in the Formal Operational Period can construct contrary-to-fact hypotheses ("if dogs were green") and reason about them. Premises are taken as "givens" regardless of whether or not they are true in experience. Formal Operational thinkers can separate the process of reasoning from the specific content, thus enabling them to solve many different types of syllogism problems. Moreover, the adolescent's own beliefs and thoughts become valid objects of inquiry. Thinking becomes just as much a subject to be reasoned about as other, more concrete problems. Mussen, Conger, Kagan, and Geiwitz (1979) reported an adolescent who said, "I was thinking about my future and then I began to think about why I was thinking about my future and then I began to think about why I was thinking about why I was thinking about my future" (p. 177).

Formal Operations are like Concrete Operations in that both are mental representations that can be reversed. Formal Operations are more advanced, though, because the representations can apply to potential as well as to actual actions, and the various reversibilities can be coordinated to permit a higher-order thinking. This coordination is derived from the basic organization principle in which isolated operations become clustered. Formal Operational thinking thus has three distinguishing characteristics: (a) generating multiple hypotheses, (b) systematic checking of all possible solutions, and (c) operating on operations.

GENERATING HYPOTHESES

Because potential hypotheses are as valid as experience-based hypotheses, Formal Operational thinkers are likely to believe that a problem might have more than one solution. Concrete Operational children may generate one solution, and if it is at all reasonable, they will stop. Formal Operational children will generate multiple alternatives. For example, if children are asked why a man was lying in the middle of the sidewalk, the Concrete Operational child might propose that the man was drunk and fell down. The Formal Operational child will consider that the man may be drunk, or had a heart attack, or was hit on the head by a robber, or is playing a joke.

SYSTEMATIC SOLUTION TESTING

The more possibilities that exist, the more children need a systematic rather than a trial-and-error approach to testing their hypotheses. The second characteristic of Formal Operational thinking is, thus, the systematic checking of all possible alternative solutions to a problem. To demonstrate this in an experimental setting, a type of chemistry problem can be presented (Inhelder & Piaget, 1958). Children are shown five colorless, odorless liquids in test tubes and are asked to discover what combination of the five will produce a yellow mixture. Concrete Operational children attempt to solve this problem through trial and error. They merely start to combine the liquids. But without an overall plan of action, one which is systematic, they soon become hopelessly lost—not remembering which combinations they have already tried and which remain to be tried. Formal Operational children proceed in a more systematic fashion, often first mixing the test tubes two at a time in a logical order (first and second, first and third,

70

first and fourth, first and fifth, second and third, and so on). Then they try combinations of three at a time, four at a time, and all five. Moreover, if Concrete Operational children stumble upon a combination which works, they will be satisfied that the problem is solved without considering that one of the liquids may be inert and hence unnecessary. Formal Operational children will continue testing even after one solution is found, isolating the relevant factors and discarding the irrelevant.

OPERATING ON OPERATIONS

Formal Operational thinkers appreciate the fact that hypothetical problems can be solved by applying the same rules as would be applied to concrete problems. In addition, they realize that the same systematic approach of isolating and testing factors can be used over a variety of contents. Therefore, they begin to generate rules which are abstract enough to cover many specific instances. Thus, the third characteristic of Formal Operations is the organization of single operations into higher-order ones. This has also been referred to as "operating on operations" in contrast to operating directly on objects as Concrete Operational children do. One way to illustrate this characteristic comes from mathematics. Given a problem such as "What number plus 20 equals twice itself?" Concrete Operational children will use the operations of addition and multiplication on various numbers in a trial-and-error way. They might, for instance, think of the number 5, insert it in the equations $5 + 20 = 25$ and $2 \times 5 = 10$, and decide that 5 was incorrect. They would continue to try other numbers in this manner until they found the correct one. Formal Operational children will develop an abstract rule, $X + 20 = 2X$, and solve the formula algebraically, $20 = 2X - X = X$. The separate operations of addition and multiplication would be combined into the higher-order algebraic operation.

One of the consequences of the ability to combine operations is that many different aspects of a problem can be dealt with simultaneously. Concrete Operational children think sequentially, considering only one aspect of a problem at a time. When several aspects can be considered together, in the Formal Operational Period, the logic of a set of beliefs can be examined.*

Adolescents are likely to consider their own beliefs about religion, politics, morality, and education in terms of logical consistency. Kagan (1971) provided the following example:

(1). God loves man.
(2). The world contains many unhappy people.
(3). If God loved man, he would not make so many people unhappy. [P. 1001]

While adolescents might resolve the inconsistency among these three statements by supposing that man is made unhappy for some hidden motive, current American adolescents tend to resolve the contradictions by denying the existence of God (often to the distress of their parents). Once one belief is challenged, all other beliefs become suspect and fair game for further attack. Adolescents are likely to challenge the adults around them to explain the inconsistencies they have suddenly found in a variety of previously accepted ideas. One can readily see where the image of an argumentative and rebellious youth comes from.

The pendulum problem

The three characteristics of Formal Operational thinking described above should be applicable to a variety of reasoning tasks. Many of Piaget's examples come from physics and mathe-

---

* Just because a person has the capacity to examine his own sets of beliefs does not mean that he always does so. This might explain why one's own children commit only harmless pranks while the neighborhood urchins engage in malicious mischief.

matics problems in inductive reasoning, in which specific facts are given and a general law must be induced. One example is referred to as the pendulum problem (Inhelder & Piaget, 1958). The setup involves a wooden stand, various lengths of string, and several weights. The experimenter suspends, one at a time, different string and weight combinations from the stand and starts the pendulum swinging by pulling the weight back to different heights and releasing it with different forces. Thus specific instances are given in the problem. Once children understand that sometimes the pendulum swings faster than at other times, they are asked to generate the law governing pendulum swinging. The correct response is that the length of the string determines the speed (short strings swing faster). Concrete Operational children generally try several combinations of weights and string lengths in a random, unsystematic fashion without proposing or testing hypotheses. Formal Operational children, on the other hand, exhibit the three characteristics of thinking outlined above. First they isolate the factors which could affect the pendulum's speed, generating multiple hypotheses about the events they have witnessed. Although the solution happens to depend on just one factor (length of string), children must eliminate the possibility that two or more factors in combination affect the pendulum's speed. Thus they must deal with multiple dimensions simultaneously. Finally, the presence of so many factors and combinations of factors requires children to systematically explore all possible solutions, not just try a few unsystematically.

The Formal Operational Period is the culmination of intellectual development for Piaget. By the time children are 15 or so, they should have all the cognitive structures necessary to do the most intellectually challenging tasks. After Formal Operations are achieved, Piaget claimed that no new kinds of structures develop; intellectual progress after adolescence consists mainly of the accumulation of new contents, or topics, for thought.

RESEARCH ISSUES

A number of researchers have challenged the accuracy of Piaget's description of the Formal Operational Period, especially children's performance on syllogism problems. In one form of the problem, valid implication reasoning, subjects must draw a correct conclusion from two premises. For example:

Premise 1: If Judy is a lawyer, then she is smart.
Premise 2: Judy is a lawyer.
Conclusion: Judy is smart.

Children who are nominally in the Concrete Operational Period (first to third grade) pass between 77 percent and 90 percent of these problems (Ennis, 1971; Kodroff & Roberge, 1975; Paris, 1973). In another syllogism form, invalid implication reasoning, subjects must avoid drawing an incorrect conclusion. For example:

Premise 1: If Judy is a lawyer, then she is smart.
Premise 2: Judy is not a lawyer.
Incorrect conclusion: Judy is not smart.
Correct conclusion: Judy may or may not be smart; one cannot say.

Adolescents, college students, and college-educated adults pass only 5 percent to 25 percent of these problems, roughly the same percentage as Concrete Operational children pass (Brainerd, 1978). Broad samples of adolescents and adults fare just as poorly on Piaget's other Formal Operational tasks (Neimark, 1975).

As the lack of empirical support became evident in the literature, Piaget (1972) advanced a number of explanations for the performance failures without really changing his conception of the underlying structures of Formal Operations. The explanation Piaget favored suggested that Formal Operational skills are more dependent on the content used in the tests than is the case in tests used for earlier stages. Extra task demands, such as knowledge of particular scientific principles, and lack of motivation or interest in the problem could produce the apparent lack of Formal Operations in adolescents and adults. Critics have argued instead that Piaget's description of the fourth period is just not appropriate for the general adult population, and they have called for new conceptualizations of mature intellectual functioning (e.g., Arlin, 1975; Greenfield, 1976; Riegel, 1973). In addition, some critics have challenged the very foundation of Piaget's theory—the idea that development proceeds by stages.

STAGE THEORY

Piaget claimed that his theory of cognitive development is a stage theory. "We have seen that there exist structures which belong only to the subject [the child], that they are built, and that this is a step-by-step process. We must therefore conclude there exist stages of development" (Piaget, 1970, p. 710). What does it mean to call a theory a stage theory? At a descriptive level, it summarizes children's capabilities at certain ages. When children at one age are regularly capable of some behaviors but not others (such as object permanence but not conservation at two years), then we can say that they are in one stage of development rather than another (Sensorimotor, not Concrete Operational). This is probably more accurate for describing cognitive development than referring to the children's chronological age, but it is of limited value because it is merely descriptive. A descriptive theory does not explain why certain behaviors change in a systematic way with age.

Stage theory gains explanatory power (and simultaneously becomes more controversial) when it proposes reasons why certain behaviors are grouped together and why those groups develop in a certain order. Piaget argued that certain be-

75

haviors constitute a stage because they share a common underlying structure, and that they develop in a particular order because the more advanced behaviors depend, in a logical way, on the more primitive ones. These requirements, of a common underlying cognitive structure and of an invariant sequence, are two of five criteria Piaget (1960) proposed to justify the identification of stages during development. Other requirements have been proposed by other researchers (e.g., Flavell, 1977) with some consensus that the following four requirements are reasonable (though not necessarily provable scientifically): (a) concurrent appearance of skills in one stage produced by a cognitive structure; (b) invariant sequence of stages; (c) qualitative differences between stages; and (d) abrupt rather than gradual transitions between stages.

Cognitive structures (Concurrence)

It seems reasonable to group behaviors together in one stage if they all depend on the same underlying cognitive structure. For example, to say that a child is in the Concrete Operational Period implies that he should be able to solve various concrete problems (e.g., conservation and class inclusion) which depend on operational thinking. Similarly, the behaviors of the Sensorimotor Period are grouped together because they use sensory and motor schemes rather than mental schemes. The same should be true for the smaller stages within the major periods; they each should have a common underlying skill which justifies grouping the various observed behaviors into the same stage. For example, if children are in the fourth stage of the Sensorimotor Period, they ought to be able to obtain any goal if the coordination of two circular reactions will solve the problem. Thus cognitive skills controlled by a common structure ought to appear concurrently rather than sequentially.

But do they? Empirical evidence for the various conservation tasks reveals consistent *decalages*—Piaget's term for the sequential appearance of logically related skills which ought to

76

have appeared simultaneously. Conservation of number develops before conservation of liquid and solid quantity (Brainerd & Brainerd, 1972; Gruen & Vore, 1972), and quantity develops before weight, which in turn develops before volume (Uzgiris, 1964). As we have seen above, the various Formal Operational tasks are also solved (or not solved) across a wide age range, which raises questions about the validity of Piaget's stage theory. The difficulty in accepting the critics' conclusion (or in accepting Piaget's theory) is one of measurement (Brainerd, 1978; Flavell, 1977).

No test is ever a pure measure of just one skill or just one underlying operation. When a test demands extra skills or knowledge, children may fail the test because they do not have that extra skill even though they may have the skill that defines the stage. In part, this measurement problem was the basis for Bower's research on object permanence and Gelman's study on conservation. Piaget referred to these extra demands to rationalize the lack of success on Formal Operational tasks by adults.

The *decalages* in conservation might also be explained by identifying components of the test which facilitate or impede solution. For example, Siegler (1981) hypothesized that conservation of number, with a small set of items in the array, develops first because children can count to verify the results of the transformation the experimenter makes. No such verification is possible when balls of clay or beakers of liquid are transformed, so conservation is slower to develop in these areas. While all of these post-hoc justifications seem reasonable, they clearly indicate the difficulty in requiring evidence of concurrent development within a stage or in finding a common cognitive structure.

Invariant sequence

A second requirement for a stage theory is to have an invariant sequence of development between stages. The very connotation of stages is a progression from less mature to more mature behaviors. If behaviors developed in a random order for each individual, a stage description would seem inappropriate. To explain the sequence, a stage theory should show why that particular sequence was the only possible one, for example, by showing that the cognitive skills of the first behaviors are prerequisites for the later behaviors. Piaget's theory aimed to do this by showing the logical necessity of the lower stage for a higher one. A child must have mental representations (in the Preoperational Period) before the representations can be reversed (in the Concrete Operational Period). They must be able to classify objects (on the multiple classification task) before they can compare two classifications (on the class inclusion test). Or, for the stages within the Sensorimotor Period, children must have individual circular reactions (stage 3) before they can coordinate those reactions to obtain a goal (stage 4).

Qualitative differences

The existence of a fixed behavioral sequence is necessary to a stage theory, but it is not sufficient for defining a stage theory because fixed sequences occur on continuous scales as well as on discontinuous (stage) ones. Therefore, a third requirement for a stage theory is that the behaviors defining a stage be qualitatively different from other stages, that is, different in kind, not just in amount (or quantity). Piaget thought that applying circular reactions to objects was qualitatively different from applying circular reactions to the infant's own body, thus warranting the designation of separate stages. The mental schemes of the Preoperational Period are qualitatively different from the behavioral schemes of the Sensorimotor Period. But what one researcher calls a qualitative change, another might reinterpret as a quantitative one.

McLaughlin (1963), for instance, claimed that the changes Piaget saw as qualitative are really quantitative changes occurring on two dimensions at the same time. These two dimensions are the abstractness in the objects of thought and the number of concepts that can be used simultaneously. As Flavell (1977) pointed out, "What looks like a qualitative change at one level of analysis may not at another" (p. 246). The closer one gets to day-to-day behavior, the more quantitative a change will look. Piaget's theory, by virtue of being more general and abstract, sees more qualitative changes.

Abrupt transitions

Finally, a stage might be identified if many behaviors change in a short period, thus forming a natural grouping. If behavioral change is slow, it becomes difficult to form meaningful separations between behaviors. Flavell (1977) commented that behavioral change will look quite abrupt if a researcher defines the onset of the stage by the first appearance of a behavior, while the change will seem very gradual if the child is required to use some behavior with ease in many different situations. Thus the definition of the onset of a stage will dictate the abruptness of the transition.

The four requirements for defining a stage theory are difficult for any theory to fulfill, and Piaget's stage theory is no exception. Whether or not cognitive development proceeds in stages remains one of the most controversial questions in developmental psychology. To get a better understanding of a nonstage theory of cognitive development, we turn our attention in the next chapter to the process approach. First, however, let us summarize the main points of Piaget's theory.

SUMMARY

Piaget proposed the functional constructs of organization and adaptation (assimilation, accommodation, and equilibration) to account for the basic ways in which children build their own cognitive structures. Since at every age, children organize and adapt to their environments, these functional aspects remain invariant over age. Although the particular balance between the functions depends on several factors (including maturation and experience), the functions themselves are viewed as unchanging. What does change with age in Piaget's system are the cognitive structures, that is, the systems of knowledge created by children's physical and mental actions on their world. Piaget identified four stages in the construction of these structures: the Sensorimotor Period, in which children have only behavioral schemes; the Preoperational Period, in which mental representations are formed; the Concrete Operational Period, in which mental representations can be reversed, yielding operations; and the Formal Operational Period, in which operations can be coordinated and applied to abstract reasoning problems, thus permitting contrary-to-fact hypothesis generation and systematic hypothesis testing.

The results of extensive research efforts have been mixed. The widespread replication of children's performance on the tasks of Piaget's first three periods is balanced by the equally widespread failure to substantiate the Formal Operational Period. Praise for the novelty and cleverness of Piaget's tasks (such as conservation and class inclusion) is balanced by criticism that the tasks are unnecessarily complicated with distracting elements. This results in a serious underestimation of children's abilities and in a more stagelike characterization of developmental change than may be warranted. The training studies and other research call into question Piaget's model of operations as an overarching general structure guiding children's problem-solving efforts. Nevertheless, the impact of Piaget's theory is without question. As Gelman (1979) summarized it, "Piaget has given us some fundamental theoretical insights as well as some fundamental phenomena" (p. 3).

3

A PROCESS APPROACH
TO COGNITIVE DEVELOPMENT

The domain of interest for cognitive psychologists is the acquisition, organization, and processing of information so that accurate (i.e., valid or useful) knowledge is achieved and can be used to solve a problem or make a decision. The preceding chapter traced Piaget's conceptualization of cognitive development. This chapter presents a different system for organizing and describing the course of cognitive development, a system arising from the American experimental research tradition in child psychology. This approach draws on experimental evidence accumulated by many investigators, working on a variety of topics, and sometimes using rats, pigeons, and even adults, rather than children, for experimental subjects. Research is, therefore, a more integral aspect of this approach. Since no one person has developed a theory that encompasses the entire experimental literature, we shall refer to this body of information as the *process approach*. The discussion is not about a single process, however, but actually covers three processes, each of which contributes to the activity we call thinking: *perception, memory,* and the *generation and testing of hypotheses.* Perception deals with the translation of raw sensory data into a form more useful for the cognitive system.

Memory concerns the storage and retrieval of information. The generation and testing of hypotheses involves proposing and evaluating possible solutions to some problem.

Generally speaking, the process approach does not utilize stages, as Piaget did, but rather views the three processes as occurring at all ages to a greater or lesser extent. For example, the number of items which children can remember and their techniques for trying to put items explicitly into storage might change with age, but at any age, memory is a process for storing and retrieving information. Similarly, the other two processes of thought are common to people of all ages, but their specific levels of functioning change, so that problem solving appears to differ with age.

The three processes have to process something. Memory has to store some event; perception has to perceive some item. These items or events are the elements of thought, the cognitive units on which the processes of thought operate. We will describe four cognitive units (schemata, symbols, concepts, and rules) before we consider the three processes which use these units.

UNITS OF THOUGHT

SCHEMATA

The first unit of thought, called a *schema* (plural: schemata), is a mental representation of events in the world. Note that this is different from *scheme* (plural: schemes), which was Piaget's term for an organized pattern of behavior.* It is intuitively obvious that adults and older children have mental representations. In response to a simple question, older, verbal children (and many adults) will produce a voluminous catalog of their knowledge. But we need to ask whether younger infants can

---

* The similarity of these terms is unfortunate but cannot be avoided. I remember schema by thinking that the last two letters start the word *map*, which is a type of representation of the world.

also represent events mentally. The answer is not easy to obtain because the behavioral repertoire of young infants is quite limited. The preverbal infant rarely responds to our questions, so we must infer what infants know by measuring phenomena we believe are determined by their knowledge. Jeffrey (1968) and McCall (1971) have suggested that a phenomenon called *habituation* could be used as an indication that infants have schemata.

In experiments using habituation, infants are presented with a stimulus, say a black circle on a white background. Infants attend visually to (look at) this stimulus. Some physiological changes also indicate that they are attending, such as changes in heart rates and breathing rates. Each time we repeat the presentation of the stimulus, however, infants spend less and less time looking at the circle. Changes in their breathing and heart rates also decrease as the stimulus is repetitively presented. The stimulus has become familiar to the infants and, in technical terminology, we would say that they have habituated to it. In nontechnical terms, we would say that they are bored. The decline in interest is not just due to general fatigue because presenting a new stimulus, say a red square on a blue background, will evoke the same magnitude of response that infants showed to the original black circle. The renewed attention is called *dishabituation*. We infer that infants have some idea of the black circle, some way of mentally representing that event, for otherwise they could not remember from one presentation to the next what they had just seen. They would not show habituation to the black circle and dishabituation to the red square unless they could represent at least the most distinctive or important elements of the two events. The term *schema* refers to this elementary memory.

The habituation experiment has been used to test systematically for which features of a stimulus are critical to an individual's schemata. The general procedure is to allow a person to habituate to a stimulus. Then one feature is changed, such as size or color or shape, and the experimenter sees if that change results in dishabituation. If it does, then that feature would be part of the person's schemata. In a typical experiment for this, Cohen, Gelber, and Lazar (1971) presented four-month-old infants with pictures of red circles for 16 trials. Then they presented 2 trials each with a new color but the old shape (green circles), a new shape but the old color (red triangles), and a new color with a new shape (green triangles). Dishabituation was greatest when both shape and color were changed, but it was also produced by the new color alone and by the new shape alone. From a later experiment, Cohen (1973) concluded that infants stored individual stimulus components (colors and shapes) rather than specific color-shape combinations because infants who had habituated to red circles and green triangles did not dishabituate to red triangles and green circles.

Cohen and Gelber (1975) reviewed research using the habituation paradigm described above and also using a preference test, in which the amount of time infants look at one or another stimulus is recorded. They concluded that "as early as 6 or 8 weeks of age a long-term exposure will produce recognition 24 hr later, and as early as 4 or 5 months of age an exposure as short as 1 or 2 min will lead to recognition 2 weeks later" (p. 368). This recognition must be controlled by schemata of the remembered stimuli. As we saw in Chapter 2, Bower's research on object permanence also addressed the issue of infant schemata. Recall that when 20-day-old infants saw a ball reappear after it had been hidden by a screen for 1½ seconds, they were not surprised, but if it had been hidden for 15 seconds, they were surprised. Both Bower and Piaget would agree that under the former condition, a schema of the ball must have been formed (and also quickly faded).

Schemata, then, are stored conceptualizations of experiences, ways of organizing or classifying prior sensory events. They are not necessarily pictorial representations (as are images), nor are they tied to language. They are probably made up of the most important or distinctive elements from an experience, perhaps like a caricature or blueprint of distinguishing features. Recall that in Bower's second experiment of object permanence, infants under 16 weeks of age used speed of movement of an object to determine its identity, not such features as size, shape, or color. Because schemata are closely related to direct sensory impressions, they are used primarily by infants and very young children. The other three units of thought (symbols, concepts, and rules) are more abstract mental representations, accessible to older children and adults. We shall now consider each of them in turn.

SYMBOLS

Symbols are arbitrary expressions or representations which stand for other things. Language is our most pervasive symbol system, and most of the sounds we produce bear only an arbitrary relation to their referents. For example, *book* is no more like the object you are currently reading than is *livre,* the French word for book. Although a few words like *buzz, chickadee,* and *bow-wow* are onomatopoetic, most words are not.

Nonlinguistic symbols include the red cross to stand for hospital aid; yellow lines to divide highway traffic flowing in opposite directions; and a red bar over a picture of a cigarette to indicate that smoking is prohibited. You might recall that symbolic functions were discussed in some detail under Piaget's Preoperational Period. The theme of that discussion was that the presence of symbolic functions can be inferred from delayed imitation, language, symbolic play, and the search for hidden objects.

CONCEPTS

Symbols generally represent specific things, including events, objects, concepts, and rules. *Concepts,* on the other hand,

characterize what is common across several different events or objects. Concepts are abstractions for the common elements among a group of schemata or symbols. If you use *car* to represent the first automobile you ever owned, then the symbol *car* represents a specific object. If, however, you use *car* to mean four-wheeled vehicles of a given size, then the symbol *car* represents the concept of car. Proper names are nearly always symbols for specific individuals (Samantha Snorkelfinger is probably one of a kind), but names can also represent concepts (John Q. Public).

The classical or componential view of concepts is that a short list of necessary and sufficient attributes completely defines a concept.* The concept of bird, for instance, might be described by the mental attribute list "animal, two wings, feathers." In order to decide if a particular instance, say a robin, fits the concept, the attributes of the robin are compared to the attributes of birds to see if they match. One should, therefore, be able to decide categorically, yes or no, if a particular instance is an example of a concept, and one example which has all and only the attributes of the concept should be just as good as another example for representing the concept. Unfortunately, many concepts do not seem to have a clear intension, and some instances are judged as better examples than others.

The lack of a clear intension can be seen with the concept *chair*. The short list of defining attributes would probably include "four-legged object with seat and back which can be sat upon." The chair shown in Figure 3-1a clearly fits these attributes. But the attribute four-legged surely is not necessary, because three-legged chairs are common. Benches would also fit the list of chair attributes, so the list is apparently not sufficient to enable us to distinguish between concepts. Although everyone can agree that the picture in Figure 3-1a is a chair, everyone would not agree just where the concept *chair* ended

---

* Note that this is identical to the definition of a class discussed in Chapter 2. If classes are particular collections of objects, concepts are particular collections of symbols.

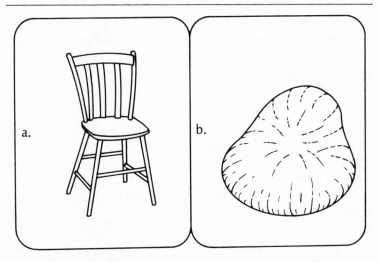

Figure 3-1. Two examples of the concept *chair*

a. A prototypical chair.
b. A beanbag chair.

and the concept *bench* began. The borders between concepts seem to be fuzzy rather than categorical.

That some instances of a concept are better than others can be demonstrated by comparing the beanbag chair shown in Figure 3-1b with the other chair in the figure. Rosch has argued that instead of being defined by a small set of necessary and sufficient attributes, concepts are defined by prototypical exemplars (Mervis & Rosch, 1981; Rosch, Mervis, Gray, Johnson, & Boyes-Braem, 1976). That is, no small set of attributes is necessary or sufficient. Rather, concept attributes are probabilistic; some subset of attributes must be present for an instance to be judged an example of a concept, but the overlap in attributes varies between any two instances of the same concept. Most concept members that are not at the fuzzy borders have a high number of shared attributes. Those exemplars which share the most attributes with other members of the conceptual class also turn out to have the fewest shared attributes with contrasting concepts and therefore make the best examples of the concept. These are called the *prototypes* for the concept. The picture of the regular chair is a good example of "chairness" while the beanbag chair is not because it does not have distinct legs. The absence of legs means that the beanbag shares one fewer attribute with other chairs and shares one more attribute with other sit-able nonchairs (such as rocks and countertops). Similarly, a robin is a "birdier" bird than a penguin.

Although we can force a list of attributes onto a concept to define it formally, with an intension, this happens developmentally after an informal, prototypical definition is created. That is, children learn the prototype of a concept before they learn about the formal defining properties separating two concepts, and they can categorize instances into concepts before they can verbalize the defining attributes for the categorization. Apparently even concepts which have clear, categorical intensions, such as "odd number," are treated prototypically because adults will rate some odd numbers, 3 and 7, as better exemplars than other odd numbers, 447 and 501, even though all of the numbers meet the definition of not being evenly divisible by two. Similarly, triangles and squares are rated as better plane geometry figures than trapezoids and ellipses (Armstrong, Gleitman, & Gleitman, as reported by Gleitman, 1981).

Because children use symbols and concepts in their speech, adults are often lulled into thinking that children are speaking "their language." That children are not is apparent when we examine four developmental changes in the use of concepts. These changes involve a concept's validity, status, accessibility, and relativity.

Four developmental changes

Validity is a measure of how well the child's use of a concept agrees with the usage by the larger social community. It has been suggested that children who do not give a conservation of number response to Piaget's tasks have concepts of number and equality different from those of adults. The adult's concepts are based on numerosity; the child's may be based on perceived length or shape. As children develop, their understanding of a concept approaches the adult meaning; the concept becomes more valid.

The second way that concept usage shows developmental change involves *status,* how precisely and exactly the concept is used. Three-year-old Bob's concept of time is likely to be vague and imprecise. When his mother tells him that they will go to the zoo "in two hours," he might go off and play for ten minutes and then ask if it is time to go. He has a valid concept of time since he knows that "in two hours" is some time in the future, but he does not know exactly how much time is indicated. Bob's ten-year-old sister Alice may be no less impatient to go, but she knows more precisely when "two hours" have elapsed.

The third change in usage involves the *accessibility* of a concept, that is, how easily children can use it in their thinking and how well they can communicate with others about it. Consider this variation on the children's game of Twenty Questions. Children are shown a set of pictures (see Figures 3-2, 3-3) and told to find out which one the experimenter has in mind by asking questions that can be answered by "yes" or "no." Young children about six years old typically just guess specific items: "Is it the zebra?" or "Is it the balloon?" When the pictures are rearranged, as in Figure 3-4, the children are more likely to ask questions involving concepts: "Is it yellow?" or "Is it a toy?" (Ault, 1973; Van Horn & Bartz, 1968). Obviously, six-year-olds have the concepts of yellow and toy, but these concepts are not as readily available as they are for older children. Increasing a concept's accessibility means increasing the chances that children will use the concept as they solve problems. An increased accessibility of concepts is also apparent in the greater verbal skills of older children who can talk about

Figure 3-2. Typical cards used in Twenty Questions

eagle	spoon	orange	dog
apple	zebra	shovel	pitcher
teapot	ball	duck	banana
kite	sprinkling can	monkey	balloon
rake	owl	wagon	bucket
cat	pear	knife	sparrow

Figure 3-3. Twenty Questions pictures in a random array

one concept by using others. For example, older children are likely to discuss the concept of justice by referring to the concepts of fairness and truth. Younger children might discuss justice in terms of the movie they could not go to because they argued with someone.

Finally, as children develop, they learn to employ concepts that are *relative* rather than absolute. If one person is taller than another, he can simultaneously be shorter than a third person. To young children who think in absolute terms, the expression "dark yellow" is contradictory because yellow is a light color. They do not understand that there are many shades of yellow, some of which are darker than others.

Differences between children's and adults' uses of concepts can also be seen in situations involving word associations. The free-association technique ("Say the first word you think of in response to my word") has been used in psychoanalysis, as a parlor game, and as a method of assessing children's language and conceptual development. Researchers have identified a progression in the types of responses children will give in the free-association situation. In the early preschool years, children will try to find a rhyme to the stimulus word, without regard for

brown eagle	brown sparrow	brown dog	brown monkey
black owl	black duck	black cat	black zebra
round apple	round orange	round ball	round balloon
yellow pear	yellow banana	yellow kite	yellow wagon
straight-handled spoon	straight-handled knife	straight-handled rake	straight-handled shovel
round-handled teapot	round-handled pitcher	round-handled bucket	round-handled sprinkling can

Figure 3-4. Twenty Questions pictures in an ordered array

the meaningfulness of their response. For example, in response to *sun,* the preschooler might say *run* or *lun.* A few years later, the child's typical response is to answer with a word that logically follows or precedes the stimulus in a sentence, such as *sun-shine* or *sun-hot.* Still later, the adult pattern emerges. That pattern is to respond with the same part of speech, frequently a synonym or antonym. To *sun,* most older children and adults respond *moon.* These adult responses are conceptually related to the stimulus word.

In addition to learning about individual concepts, children must learn to relate two or more of them. This results in rules, the fourth unit of thought.

RULES

Rules are statements which specify the relationship between two or more concepts. We have several different dimensions for describing rules. One distinction is between formal and informal rules. Informal rules express relationships which are generally true ("Mommy is nice") but which can be violated

("Mommy won't let me watch TV now"). Formal rules are always true under certain specified conditions. In base-10 arithmetic, $2 + 2 = 4$. Conservation of number can be expressed by the formal rule: number changes only when something is added or subtracted, not when shape is manipulated.

Language acquisition illustrates two important features of rule learning. First, rules simplify enormously the task of generating a solution to a problem. In forming proper grammatical sentences, consider trying to learn by rote the past tense form of all verbs. Without a rule, children would never know how to conjugate a verb they had not heard before. Second, informal rules are common. Grammatical rules are seldom always applicable. Rather, they seem made to be violated. The following pattern is typical of grammar-rule acquisition (Kuczaj, 1978). First, situations are handled idiosyncratically, without rules. Children learn some past tense verbs such as "went" and "came," apparently by rote. Then they appear to know that a rule can govern past tenses ("Add *ed* to the present tense") because they begin to produce correct regular forms (e.g., I walk; I walked), and they overgeneralize the rule in many situations (I goed; I comed). Eventually these overgeneralized cases drop out. If children do not know the proper form for a particular verb, even if they know the verb is irregular, they may produce an incorrect but rule-governed form. Recall the eight-year-old who said, "All you did was spreaded them out." In fact, even college students, who know that "bring" is an irregular verb (and will not say "bringed"), will incorrectly generalize from such words as "sing" to produce the past tense "brang."

In addition to being categorized as formal or informal, rules can be classified as transformational or nontransformational. Transformational rules prescribe an action to be taken on the related concepts or specify the outcome of some action. The following statements are examples of transformational rules: "Mix flour, water, and eggs to make a cake" and "Multiply the length by the width to obtain the area of a rectangle." Nontransformational rules, like "Fire is hot" and "A square has four equal sides," do not prescribe any action. One major developmental change in the use of rules is to acquire more rules, both formal and informal, and to make these rules more accurate. A second major developmental change is a shift from using no rules or only nontransformational ones to using transformational rules.

Conceptual sorting test

Despite the increase in transformational rules, nontransformational rules remain quite common and come in many different forms. One way to relate two concepts is a class inclusion relation. If one concept is the superordinate for another (e.g., furniture is the superordinate concept for chair), the relationship is *categorical-superordinate*. Three other relationships are *functional-locational*, in which the concepts share a location; *functional-relational*, in which one concept acts on the other; and *analytic*, in which both concepts share a detail or feature. The Conceptual Sorting Test was designed to measure children's preferences for relating concepts (Kagan, Rosman, Day, Albert, & Phillips, 1964). In this test, children are shown sets of pictures, each containing three items. They are asked to pick the two things which "are alike in some way" and to explain the basis for the choice. One set of pictures from the test shows a man, a watch, and a ruler. A categorical-superordinate grouping would join the watch and the ruler because both are measuring devices. A functional-relational response would group the man and the watch because the man wears the watch. If a child groups the watch and the ruler because both are found in the house, a functional-locational response is indicated. An analytic response, based on similarity of some detail, would group the watch and the ruler because both have numbers. Thus the reasons given by children for their particular groupings are important for determining how children relate concepts to each other.

94

The first research using the Conceptual Sorting Test with American children seemed to indicate an age-related change in the basis of the sorting (Kagan et al., 1964). Preschool children preferred to make functional-relational groupings whereas older children formed categorical-superordinate and analytic groupings. Extensions of this work to other cultures led to some surprising results. Glick (1969) presented Kpelle (West African) rice farmers with an array of familiar objects and asked them to sort the objects into groups that belonged together. The farmers tended to sort on the basis of the functional-relational dimension. For example, a gazelle and a leaf were placed together because the gazelle eats the leaf. The farmers formed very few categorical-superordinate groups, such as a gazelle and a zebra because both are animals. While some investigators might have drawn the conclusion that Kpelle adults were at a low level of cognitive development (equal to American children), Glick was not convinced that Kpelle adults were any less developed than American adults. Therefore, he asked them why they had sorted as they did. They replied that "this was the clever way to do it, the way that made 'Kpelle sense.'" Glick then asked them to sort the items the way a stupid Kpelle might, and they made perfect categorical-superordinate categories comparable to those made by American adults.

Obviously, each culture has its own definition of cleverness and teaches its people to respond in the clever manner. Furthermore, other tests with American children have systematically varied some aspects of the testing situation, such as whether the stimuli were pictures or words, and obtained different proportions of categorical, analytic, and functional responses (Olver & Hornsby, 1966). The conclusion seems to be that children learn several rules for relating concepts to each other, but not in any specific age-related manner.

In summary, cognitive processes operate with four units of thought: schemata, symbols, concepts, and rules. Several major shifts occur in children's use of these units. One such developmental change is from using primarily schemata to using symbols, concepts (especially language), and rules. In another change, concepts gain increased validity, status, and accessibility, and children learn to use them relatively as well as absolutely. A third shift with age involves the particular rule (formal or informal; transformational or nontransformational) children will use to solve a problem. These developmental changes in the units of thought are closely related to the development of the processes of thought, which we shall examine in the next section.

PROCESSES OF THOUGHT

It is virtually impossible to discuss as complex a phenomenon as thinking in a single unit; but it can be misleading to separate the phenomenon into its components, especially when the pieces are so interwoven. In this chapter, thinking is divided into three processes—perception, memory, and the generation and testing of hypotheses—but you should remember that the distinction between them frequently blurs.

PERCEPTION

Our physical sensory receptors for vision, hearing, touch, and so forth make information contained in the environment available for further processing, but assigning meaning to that information depends, in part, on perception. Two major views of perception have guided research on *how* we perceive. After we outline these two views, we will examine the end product of perception, *what* we perceive.

Enrichment theory

According to the *enrichment* (or *schema*) theory, physical stimulation from the sensory receptors is relatively poor in information value and cannot be interpreted without considerable ad-

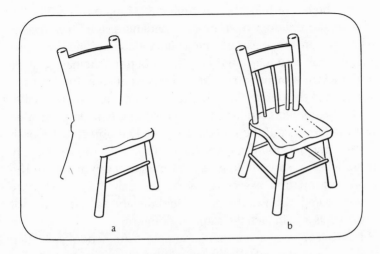

Figure 3-5. Two drawings of a chair

a. The older child is likely to recognize the partially completed picture as a chair.
b. The younger child must see a more complete picture to recognize it.

ditional information enriching the sensations. The additional information can come from biases and expectations governed by prior experiences similar to the current one and from memory, in the form of prior schemata concerning the object or event. Both sources of additional information predict that older children will have faster and more accurate perceptions than younger children. Because older children have experienced more than younger children, they will have more information to choose from to enrich a current stimulus. If information is incomplete, older children will have more accurate expectations for what will complete it. For example, they have a higher success rate in identifying a picture when only parts of the drawing are made visible (Gollin, 1960, 1962) (see Figure 3-5 for an illustration of partial and complete drawings).

The enrichment theory proposes that each time an object is perceived, a small amount of information is added to the previous schema for that object (Bruner, 1957; Vernon, 1955). Because older children have more experiences, they have better schemata (in the sense of being more detailed and more accurate) than younger children. These better schemata can be retrieved from memory to add to the current stimulus, thus enriching current perception. Any task such as discriminating between two objects requires comparing the schemata associated with each object. If the schemata for the two objects are identical, the person should not be able to distinguish between them. If the schemata are different, a discrimination can be made. The more information associated with the schemata, the more likely a comparison of them will yield the correct decision (that the objects are, in fact, the same or different).

Let us consider a common example from school in which children are presented with the letters *b, d, p,* and *q.* For younger children who have had little exposure to letters, identical schemata might be formed for each stimulus, as shown in Figure 3-6a. With more experience, children should form the second set of schemata, shown in Figure 3-6b. This set has the added information that the loops are at the top or bottom of the straight line. This set would not allow the children to distinguish *b* from *d* or *p* from *q,* but it would allow them to distinguish *b* or *d* from *p* or *q.* Finally, children might construct the schemata in Figure 3-6c, adding the information about the left-right orientation of the loop relative to the line. Now all four letters can be distinguished.

One point about this example needs to be clarified. The drawings in Figure 3-6c have been oversimplified and could give the incorrect impression that the schemata are exact images of the stimuli, but that is not the intention. Schemata are not simple graphic images.

Differentiation theory

The alternative *differentiation* or *distinctive features* theory proposes that sensory stimulation is a very rich source of infor-

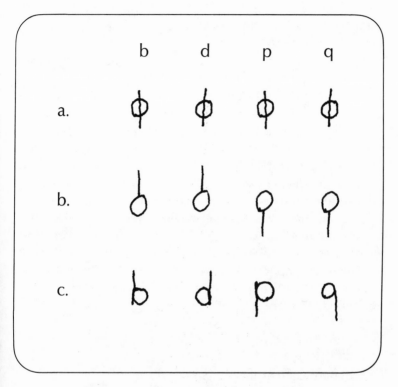

Figure 3-6. Schemata of the four letters b, d, p, and q

mation, instead of a very poor one. The process of perception is to extract the distinctive features or the invariant patterns contained within the complex, variable flow of stimulation (Gibson, 1969; Gibson & Levin, 1975). Three principles govern this view of perception: the differentiation of distinctive features by abstraction, the ignoring of irrelevant information, and the systematic search for relevant information. The last two principles are facets of attention and will be considered shortly. The first principle is the one which most clearly distinguishes the differentiation theory from the enrichment theory. It proposes that each time a person perceives an object, new features or relationships can be detected which were not noticeable before. Practice or prior experience teaches a person which features or patterns of features are distinctive and therefore critical for identification of the object. Perceptions thus become more differentiated, increasing the degree of correspondence between the potential stimulus information and the perception of that information.

Let us return to the example of learning the four letters to see how the differentiation theory interprets children's acquisition of this discrimination. Children with little prior exposure to letters might decide that the distinctive features of these stimuli were the presence of a line and a loop, as diagrammed in Figure 3-7a. These two characteristics would not help distinguish the four letters in the set. With more experience, children might select the position of the loop at the top or bottom of the line as an important feature (see Figure 3-7b). Finally, the feature of left-right orientation for the loop would be noticed (see Figure 3-7c), and all four letters could be distinguished.

Attention

Both the enrichment theory and the differentiation theory acknowledge the importance of the mechanism of attention in perception and seem to accept the same account of it, with a few exceptions which will be explained below. Both ignoring irrelevant information and deliberately scanning for relevant information are components of active attention. Gibson called these two components central and peripheral attention, respectively (Gibson & Levin, 1975). Attention does not begin with these components, however. Rather, it seems to have a passive nature first.

In early infancy, attention is characterized by such terms as *captured* and *stimulus-controlled* because certain stimuli automatically trigger an orienting reaction. Just as the behavioral reflexes of the first Sensorimotor stage initiated motor re-

a. b → straight line and loop

d → straight line and loop

p → straight line and loop

q → straight line and loop

b. b → loop at bottom of line

d → loop at bottom of line

p → loop at top of line

q → loop at top of line

c. b → loop at bottom-right of line

d → loop at bottom-left of line

p → loop at top-right of line

q → loop at top-left of line

Figure 3-7. Feature sets associated with the letters *b, d, p,* and *q*

sponses, the orienting reflexes engage the visual system.* Allik and Valsiner (1980) proposed that this is "a specific evolutionary adaptation that allows the motorically very immature human infant to extract the kind of stimulation from the environment that is necessary for the functional development of the visual system" (p. 6). Later, a more voluntary side of attention develops, so infants can control what they look at and how long they look (just as many reflexes give way to voluntary motor movements).

* We will use vision to illustrate attention since most research has been done with that sensory modality.

Cohen (1973) distinguished between two phases of attention: attention getting and attention holding. In early infancy, what gets attention in infants is a function of the size and movement of objects, while what holds their attention is a function of the complexity and familiarity of the pattern. We have encountered the importance of familiarity or novelty of a pattern twice before, when we discussed the habituation phenomenon under the topic of schemata and when we mentioned the "moderate novelty principle" as a basic assumption of the cognitive perspective. The measure of the formation of a schema was the change in attention that occurred as a stimulus was repeatedly presented. If an object continues to match the infant's schema, no new information can be extracted, so attention drops off. If the object is changed, dishabituation (renewed attention) occurs. Yet, if the novel object is too discrepant from old schemata, the infant will have no way of understanding it and so will not attend to it.

The enrichment theory would describe this by saying that no old schemata will be added to the new stimulus and so it will be relatively meaningless. Differentiation theory would say that the distinctive features of the new stimulus would not be detected. (And Piaget would describe the phenomenon in terms of the inability to assimilate and accommodate to the stimulus.) All of these explanations are circular, though, because we measure the degree of discrepancy by the amount of attention a child shows, and we claim the amount of attention is dictated by the degree of discrepancy. Nevertheless, data supporting the habituation evidence comes from measuring infants' preferences for certain stimuli, as determined by the length of time they will look at one stimulus compared to another. When the stimuli are pictures of human faces, the data seem to fit the following pattern:

> Initially, presumably before the infant has had sufficient experience to have developed a schema for human faces, there is no preference for either regular or scrambled face stimuli. However, at around 4 months, when a schema for faces is

102

> inferred to be developing, infants come to prefer regular faces, which presumably provide a moderate degree of discrepancy from the developing schema. Once the face schema becomes firmly established, regular faces become too familiar and scrambled faces present an optimum amount of discrepancy. [Cohen, DeLoache, & Strauss, 1979, p. 425]

Central attention   As the infant's attention becomes less captured and more voluntary, the central and peripheral components can be noted. _Central attention,_ also called selective attention, refers to the active selection of some information and the rejection or ignoring of the rest. The amount of physical stimulation available to a person is truly overwhelming. Sights, sounds, odors, and touches are continually available for our sensory organs, yet we seem to take notice of only a fraction of them because we have the ability to attend selectively. At a very noisy cocktail party, we can listen to the one conversation directed at us while we ignore all the others. Selective attention is also demonstrated when children are so engrossed in a game that they do not hear their mother calling them (although parents might prefer the explanation that children show selective oblivion).

The constructivist or enrichment theory explanation is that the available information is just not processed. As Neisser explained it, "The perceiver ignores information simply by not doing anything with it. Such information is just not perceived in the same sense that objects currently lying on my desk are just not being grasped and my pipe is not currently being smoked" (1979, p. 203). The differentiation view is that information is filtered out, actively rejected after a minimal amount of processing has indicated that it is not desired.

Although children of all ages exhibit some selective attention, the capability becomes refined with increased age, permitting the older child to eliminate highly attractive distractions better than the younger child. An experimental task which shows the superior selective attention of older children was developed by Stroop (1935). In one variation of the task, children are shown a card printed with various color names. Sometimes the names are printed in black ink, and sometimes they are printed in different colors. Thus, the word *red* might be printed in yellow letters. The children are asked either to name the color of the letters (ignoring the word) or to read the word (ignoring the colors of the letters). The words are a powerful distracting cue, especially for the younger children, who make more naming errors than older children when they are asked to name the color of the letters. Santostefano and Paley (1964) have demonstrated the same phenomenon using normally or incongruously colored pictures of fruit.

Because older children are not as distracted by irrelevant information, their attention span is longer. Thus the length of time that a child will remain at a task increases with age. For this reason, teachers often program only 10 minutes of an academic activity with nursery school children, 30 minutes with grade school children, and 60 minutes with high school students. But as you know from your own experiences, some activities are more interesting than others, so the length of time you attend to them varies accordingly. Most children will play outside much longer than they will play the piano. An infant will play with a rattle longer than will a college professor (at least, most college professors), but if one takes into consideration the appeal of an activity for an individual, then the older child's attention span is, on the whole, longer.

Attention should not necessarily be focused on just one thing. It is useful in problem solving to be able to shift attention between various aspects of the task. As children gain more control over voluntary central attention, they increase the speed with which they can redirect their attention. A very rapid shift in the focus of attention may result in the perception of a relationship that might otherwise not be apparent. Perhaps this is equivalent to saying that a person can hold two facets of a task in mind simultaneously. Piaget explained successful performance on the class inclusion problem by stating that children attended to both the parts and the whole at the same time. An alternative explanation is that successful children shift their attention between the parts and the whole so rapidly that they perceive a new relationship between the two.

The pattern that emerges for children's central attention is an increasing ability to take the demands of the task into consideration. In tasks where one stimulus dimension is relevant and the rest are irrelevant, older children are more successful at ignoring the irrelevant (they focus more). In tasks where two or more dimensions are relevant, older children tend to split their attention across dimensions while younger children do not consistently attend to both. Thus, older children are more responsive to the demands of the task (Shepp, Burns, & McDonough, 1980).

Peripheral attention   Attention is considered _peripheral_ when it is used to scan the environment, to explore for important or relevant information. Peripheral attention can be seen for the sense of touch by the manual exploration of an object. Young infants clutch an object; older children systematically run their fingers over the contours (Gibson, 1970). With vision, scanning can be detected if children's eye movements are carefully photographed. Major developmental advances occur in such areas as selecting the more informative parts of a picture for fixation, covering the entire display, comparing parts more systematically, and maintaining a scanning strategy across changes in the stimulus (Day, 1975).

What is perceived

The process of perception involves obtaining meaning from sensory stimulation. What is the end product of that process? According to Gibson's differentiation theory, we perceive (a) distinctive features of static objects, (b) invariant relations of events over time, and (c) relations between distinctive features or between events (Gibson & Levin, 1975). Distinctive features of objects were discussed under the topic of habituation and included such features as size, shape, color, and movement. The invariance of events over time can be exemplified by the perception of a closing door. We see one door moving in time, not a series of discrete stationary doors. The ability to perceive relations between features or events (or both) enables the perception of spatial relations (e.g., one thing is to the left of another) and two-dimensional representations (e.g., pictures of three-dimensional objects). Pattern perception enables a person to identify one particular example from a class of similar objects. For example, the avid birdwatcher can identify the pattern which is the yellow-bellied sapsucker even in a tree full of other birds. Relational perception also facilitates the identification of symbolic codes. The two most prominent symbolic codes that children must learn are the phonemes which make up spoken language and the graphemes of written language. A girl must perceive the difference in sounds between *Tad* and *Dad* when she has to decide whether to throw a ball to her brother or her father. Similarly, she must perceive the difference between *b* and *d* to read *bed* and *deb* correctly.

What is perceived changes with experience and maturation. In general, more features are distinguished and more higher-order relationships are identified with increasing exposure to a stimulus. In infancy, a clear developmental trend has been identified (Cohen, 1979). It begins with the primitive ability of newborns (up to the age of about one and one-half months) to detect edges, that is, a relationship between a figure and its ground. Between two and four months, infants perceive the relations among edges (which is, thus, the perception of angles), and they process simple forms. From five to seven months, they perceive relations among forms, thus producing simple pattern perception. This allows, among other things, the recognition of one human face as distinct from others.

We have seen that differentiation theory and enrichment theory provide different interpretations of some phenomena and parallel interpretations of others. Some psychologists believe the two theories are complementary rather than conflicting. Stevenson (1972) offered the explanation that people can both build up a schema and pick out the distinctive features of a stimulus. When children must make an identification of one stimulus, they can compare it with various schemata and pick the best match. When they must distinguish among several stimuli simultaneously, they can isolate the distinctive features. Recall that schemata are not exact images of a stimulus. It may be that "schemata are composed of distinctive features and . . . when many distinctive features have been stored, one has a 'refined' schemata" (Caldwell & Hall, 1970, p. 7).

Other psychologists focus on the differences between the theories. Lewis and Brooks (1975) pointed out that in differentiation theory, finding distinctive features precedes the development of a schema whereas in enrichment theory, a schema is built first and later refined by adding distinctive elements. Cohen et al. (1979) concluded that "taken as a whole, the evidence does not unequivocally support any one global theory" (p. 428).

No matter what theory of perception eventually proves to be true, it is clear that perception does not function in isolation of the other processes of thought. Perception and memory are particularly intertwined since perceptions are stored in memory (be they in the form of schemata or relations or distinctive features), so we turn next to the process of memory.

MEMORY

When we encode and store some aspects of an experience and then, after a period of time, retrieve part of that stored representation, we have engaged the process of memory. Many of our memory efforts, especially in a school setting, are deliberate. We know ahead of time that some information will need to be retrieved later, so we employ deliberate strategies to facilitate that later memory attempt. Other memories are incidental by-products of some other cognitive activity. For example, we may have the task of sorting pictures of birds and trees into two classes, and afterward, we are asked to recall the pictures. Our memory for the pictures is incidental to the primary sorting task and hence nondeliberate or involuntary. The distinction between deliberate and involuntary memory has recently been accentuated by the publication of some Soviet research on children's memory and by the formulation of the levels of processing model of adult memory, which challenges the traditional multistore model. We will use the dichotomy between deliberate and involuntary memory as an organizing principle as we describe children's memory development.

Deliberate memory

Whenever a person deliberately encodes a list of words, a collection of pictures or objects, the spatial location of items, and so forth, with the explicit intention of retrieving that information later, memory is the goal of the cognitive activity. By far the majority of memory research has concerned deliberate memory and has been set in the theoretical framework of the multistore model of Atkinson and Shiffrin (1968). The multistore model has two basic components: (a) three structural storage systems (or stores) which are "hard-wired" into the brain and (b) "control processes" which are factors influencing the selection and maintenance of information within and between the structural stores (Hagen & Stanovich, 1977). We will first consider the three structural stores which are called the sensory, short-term, and long-term stores. Then we will turn to three control processes: strategies, metamemory, and general world knowledge.

<u>Sensory store</u>   The *sensory store* is the briefest of the three storage systems, lasting only about $1/4$ of a second. To demonstrate the existence of this store, Sperling (1960) used a device called a tachistoscope to show subjects a stimulus for a very brief period (50 msec). The stimulus in this particular experi-

ment consisted of nine letters, arranged in three rows of three each. After the letters flashed off, subjects would typically report four or five of the nine possible letters. Two explanations for this level of performance seemed probable. Either subjects had seen four or five letters and reported everything in their memory, or the subjects had seen all nine letters but forgotten some of them before they could report them all. The latter hypothesis was supported when Sperling changed the procedure slightly. He prearranged a signal system with the subjects so that a high tone indicated they should report the top row of letters, a middle tone indicated they should report the middle row, and a low tone indicated the bottom row. Then, *after* the visual stimulus was turned off, one tone was played. Subjects were able to report the one appropriate row quite easily. Thus they must have seen all nine letters. When the tone sounded, they scanned their sensory memory store and reported the letters in that row. The memory image must fade very quickly though, because even a delay of $1/4$ second in sounding the tone resulted in much poorer performance.

When children from the age of five years and older have been contrasted with adults, few if any differences have been found in either the amount of information available to the sensory store or the rate of decay of information in it (see reviews by Hoving, Spencer, Robb, & Schulte, 1978; Kail & Siegel, 1977). The procedure Sperling used is obviously unsuitable for infants, and we have no other way for testing their sensory store. It does not appear likely, however, that interesting developmental changes will be found in the sensory store. Since we know that our memories last longer than $1/4$ second, a distinction can apparently be drawn between the sensory store and the two longer-lasting ones.

Short-term store   Memories in *short-term store* last longer than sensory memories, up to 30 seconds, but they are also transitory in the sense that information can be lost during that time. We use the short-term store when we need to remember a phone number just long enough to dial it, or to remember the purchase price of an item just long enough to get out our money. The features of short-term store have been explored with two different retrieval situations, recognition and recall.

In its simplest form, recognition is that "gee, your face looks familiar" or "don't I know this from somewhere" feeling we get when we reencounter a person or object. In a more complex situation, recognition involves choosing one stimulus from a set as the solution to a problem, as students do on multiple choice tests. The possible alternatives are limited, and the person merely has to recognize the correct one. In contrast, in recall situations, a person must generate the stored representation for himself. Fill-in-the-blank and essay tests are common recall situations in school.

In laboratory experiments, the two types of retrieval can be compared for children of many ages. In one experiment, for example, 4-year-olds and 10-year-olds were shown 12 pictures to be remembered. At both ages, the children could select the 12 pictures out of a set of 100. On a recall test, however, when they were asked to name the 12 pictures they had seen, the 4-year-olds could recall only 2 or 3 pictures whereas the 10-year-olds could recall about 8 (Kagan, Klein, Haith, & Morrison, 1973). When even younger children are first shown 18 objects and then asked to pick them out of a set of 36 objects, 4-year-olds are correct 92 percent of the time and 2-year-olds are correct 81 percent (Perlmutter & Myers, 1974). Thus short-term memory tested by recognition is quite good across all ages, but when tested by recall, striking developmental changes are seen. If adults try to remember a random sequence of digits or nonsense syllables, they usually recall about 7 items (Miller, 1956). Five-year-olds recall at most about 5 items, and younger children recall even fewer. Does this difference represent a capacity difference in the structural aspects of the short-term store? Researchers initially interpreted the data in that way, but the recognition data argue against it, and now researchers are pointing instead to age changes in the use of strategies (a control process), such as chunking information into larger, meaningful units (Chi, 1976, 1978). This point will be discussed again when we examine the control processes.

Long-term store   Long-term store is different from the sensory and short-term stores in at least two important ways. First, its capacity is clearly enormous. All the memories we have of our childhood, of last year, of last week, of language, and so on are represented in long-term store. Second, items do not automatically disappear from the long-term store in a short period of time. Whether items can ever be permanently lost or are just temporarily inaccessible is a long-standing, unresolved topic of debate.

Does the structure of the long-term store change with age? That is, do children and adults differ in the capacity of long-term store or in the rate of losing information from it? Everyone knows that adults and older children have much better memories than do younger children. But researchers have a hard time deciding whether to attribute the changes to structural development or to the control processes, especially the strategies for encoding and retrieving information. Some evidence of structural development is that neurons in the brain continue to grow for as long as seven years postnatally. That growth is seen in the myelinization of axons and branching of dendrites which is correlated with memory (Kesner & Baker, 1980), but the specific effects of biological brain maturation on memory performance are not well specified. Moreover, three control processes are good candidates for explaining long-term memory performance differences between children and adults. These control processes are (a) deliberate strategies for encoding and retrieving, (b) knowledge about memory situations and memorizing (called metamemory), and (c) general world knowledge.

Strategies

> Piglet had got up early that morning to pick himself a bunch
> of violets; and when he had picked them and put them in a

111

pot in the middle of his house, it suddenly came over him that nobody had ever picked Eeyore a bunch of violets, and the more he thought of this, the more he thought how sad it was to be an Animal who had never had a bunch of violets picked for him. So he hurried out again, saying to himself, "Eeyore, Violets," and then "Violets, Eeyore," in case he forgot, because it was that sort of day. [Milne, 1961a, p. 86]

Strategies such as rehearsal, imagery, and chunking are deliberate procedures for trying to put information into the memory stores or to retrieve that information. These are "control processes" because they are under a person's voluntary control. *Rehearsal* is an encoding strategy which enhances both short-term and long-term memory. If we need to keep information in the short-term store, just long enough to perform some action (as Piglet did), we can repeat it over and over to ourselves in a rote fashion. This type of rehearsal maintains the information in the short-term store, but it is not very useful for transferring the information into the long-term store. A second type of rehearsal, which is repeating the information while thinking about it more, or elaborating on it, does increase the chances of putting the information into long-term store. Children under about seven years do not spontaneously use either type of rehearsal, which is one reason why their memory performance is worse than that of older children (Flavell, Beach, & Chinsky, 1966). When young children are instructed to rehearse, they can do so, and their recall improves correspondingly (Keeney, Cannizzo, & Flavell, 1967).

In a study of rehearsal using a serial recall task, Kingsley and Hagen (1969) first taught some nursery school children animal labels for nonsense figures drawn on cards like those shown in Figure 3-8. Then the children played a game like "Concentration." One at a time, five cards were shown to a child and then turned face down in a row. Next a cue card, identical to one of the stimulus cards, was presented (see Figure 3-9). The child's task was to select the matching card from the face-down row, thereby indicating memory for the serial position of the card.

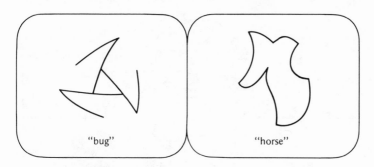

Figure 3-8. Two nonsense figures and their labels, from an experiment by Kingsley and Hagen (1969)

The experimental group relevant to this discussion was required to label each stimulus card as it was presented and to rehearse these labels, starting from the beginning of the row, after each new card was presented. In remembering the location of the matching card, children in this group performed significantly better than children in two other groups who labeled the cards as they were presented but did not rehearse or who neither labeled nor rehearsed the cards. The superiority of the subjects who rehearsed was most apparent when the matching card had been presented first (and therefore had to be kept in memory for the longest time). The authors concluded that nursery school children do not spontaneously name or repeat items to be remembered in a memory task, but if they are helped to do so, their memory scores improve.

Not only are older children more likely to use rehearsal than younger children, but the way they rehearse also becomes more effective with age. Ornstein, Naus, and Liberty (1975) asked third-, sixth-, and eighth-grade children to rehearse aloud in the free times between presentations of an 18 word list. Third graders tended to rehearse each word in isolation, or perhaps with one other word, whereas the sixth and eighth graders rehearsed four or five words as a set. Table 3-1 shows the first four words of the list and typical responses by a third

113

Figure 3-9. Procedure in Kingsley and Hagen's experiment

a. Experimenter presents third card to subject.
b. Experimenter presents cue card. Subject must turn over middle card to be correct.

TABLE 3-1

TYPICAL REHEARSAL PROTOCOLS
OF UNRELATED WORDS*

Word presented	Third-grade subject	Eighth-grade subject
1. Yard	Yard, yard, yard, yard, yard	Yard, yard, yard
2. Cat	Cat, cat, cat, cat, yard	Cat, yard, yard, cat
3. Man	Man, man, man, man, man	Man, cat, yard, man, yard, cat
4. Desk	Desk, desk, desk, desk	Desk, man, yard, cat, man, desk, cat, yard

* Adapted from Ornstein, Naus, & Liberty (1975)

and eighth grader. Notice that the third grader is speaking a word just as often as the eighth grader; it is the quality, not the quantity, of rehearsal that is helpful in making the older children's recall better.

Rehearsal is not even a preferred mnemonic strategy until children are about in fifth grade. Kreutzer, Leonard, and Flavell (1975) interviewed children from the kindergarten, first, third, and fifth grades, asking questions about what the children knew about their own memory processes.* For example, the children were asked:

> (1) If you wanted to phone your friend and someone told you the phone number, would it make any difference if you called right away after you heard the number or if you got a drink of water first? (2) Why? (3) What do you do when you want to remember a phone number? [P. 9]

Even some of the kindergarten children knew that some things could be forgotten rapidly. By first grade, over half of the chil-

* This is also an aspect of metamemory, which we will consider in more detail later.

115

dren said they should phone first or else they might forget the number. In response to the third part of the question, the most common strategy offered for aiding memory relied on external prompts, either writing down the number or having someone else (i.e., Mother) remind them of it. The following answer from a third grader reflects at attempt to devise a self-generated prompt.

> Say the number is 633-8854. Then what I'd do is—say that my number is 633, so I won't have to remember that, really. And then I would think, now I've got to remember 88. Now I'm 8 years old, so I can remember, say, my age two times. And then I say how old my brother is, and how old he was last year. And that's how I'd usually remember that phone number. [Is that how you would most often remember a phone number?] Well, usually I write it down. [P. 11]

Only at fifth grade did some of the children think of verbal rehearsal as a deliberate memory strategy. They knew that they should repeat the number several times, and that the last four numbers would be harder to remember than the first three, which might be the same exchange as their own number.

A second encoding strategy for improving deliberate memory is *imagery,* creating a distinctive picture which either includes the item to be remembered or symbolizes it. If you need to remember that the term *Concrete Operations* refers to Piaget's third period of development, you might imagine *three* surgeons *operating* on a slab of *concrete* (see Figure 3-10). Imagery can be used more easily for some memory tasks than others because some terms evoke images more readily. For example, most Americans probably form a similar image of the Washington Monument (see Figure 3-11), but their images of freedom depend on their perspectives (see Figure 3-12). Like rehearsal, imagery is not spontaneously used by young children, but when an experimenter tells them to generate images, kindergarten and even nursery school children can do so, and their memory subsequently improves (see Reese, 1977, for a review of this literature).

116

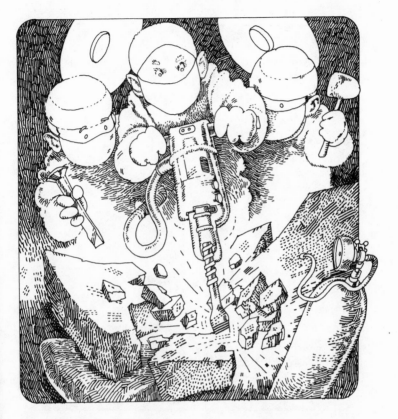

Figure 3-10. An image of three doctors operating on concrete, to symbolize Piaget's third period of development,
the Concrete Operational Period

Both encoding and retrieval can be improved by a strategy
called *chunking* (Miller, 1956). Chunking involves finding some
higher-order category to which several of the items belong and
organizing storage and retrieval of information according to
these categories. Let us say, for example, that children needed
to remember the following list: zebra, cow, dog, pig, horse,
balloon, kite, wagon, ball, yo-yo, car, truck, plane, bus, and
boat. If they tried to remember the list without any organizing

Figure 3-11. Image of the Washington Monument

principle, they would probably only recall 5 to 9 words, the limit imposed by short-term store. If they recognized, however, that the list included five animals, five toys, and five vehicles, they might succeed in remembering 12 to 15 words. Chunking the information into higher-order groups makes it easier to handle by providing an organized method for remembering. Kindergarten, first-, and third-grade children do not spontaneously chunk items either while they examine the stimulus ma-

118

Figure 3-12. Images of freedom

terials or later during recall. With instruction   nking,
however, even the kindergarten children can d   their
memory scores improve considerably (Moely,   lwes,
& Flavell, 1969).

In the studies cited above, we have seen a   ittern
where younger children apparently do not think   lelib-
erate strategies to help them remember, but when they are induced by instructions or other task constraints to use strategies,
their memory performance improves. Does the lack of strategies account for all of the memory differences between younger
and older children? Apparently not. First, even with training in
the use of the strategies, younger children's memory performance often does not improve all the way to adult levels. Second, as soon as the experimenter stops prompting the children
to use the strategy, they stop using it. These two facts suggest
that other factors are responsible for younger children's poorer
memory. In particular, children's knowledge about memory
(called metamemory) and their general world knowledge are
probably additional sources of developmental changes in
memory.

Metamemory One factor which could affect memory performance is knowledge about memory itself. Flavell (1971) has
called this _metamemory,_ while Brown (1975) used the phrase
knowing about knowing. One example has already been presented under the topic of rehearsal, where children were asked
whether a time delay makes it harder to remember a phone
number. Flavell and Wellman (1977) provided a review of the
current research on this topic, and this section is based on their
presentation.

Metamemory can be classified into four categories. One is
sensitivity, which is knowing when to exert an effort to retrieve
information or to prepare for some future retrieval. If you were
asked to describe the clothing a friend wore yesterday, you
would realize that a deliberate retrieval search is called for, but
you also probably realize that you will not find the answer be-

120

cause you did nothing yesterday to help store this information. Yet, if you had been told yesterday that today you would be asked about your friend's dressing habits, you would have been sensitive to the need to prepare for this. No one has yet studied when or how young children deal with unexpected retrieval requests, except to document that they can smile very sweetly, look very puzzled, and say, "I don't know." If forewarned about a memory situation, children as young as three years will profit from the warning, as indicated by their remembering more than children who are told nothing or who are told merely to wait between the stimulus presentation and the retrieval time (Acredelo, Pick, & Olsen, 1975; Wellman, Ritter, & Flavell, 1975).

The knowledge that you probably will not remember your friend's clothing without forewarning illustrates a second category of metamemory, *person variables*. This includes knowing whether you are a good or poor rememberer compared to other people or compared to yourself at other times or in other situations. Even five-year-olds know their relative standings in memory situations; they are better than two-year-olds but not as good as older children and adults. Five-year-olds are not, however, very accurate in assessing their own memory in an absolute sense. They overestimate their memory span and underestimate their readiness for recall (Flavell, Friedrichs, & Hoyt, 1970).

The third category of metamemory, *task variables,* includes knowledge of what items are to be memorized and the format for item presentation. By kindergarten, children know that it is easier to memorize familiar items than unfamiliar ones and that lengthening a list increases its difficulty. On the other hand, not until the third to fifth grades do children realize that learning a list of words embedded in a story is easier than learning the list in isolation, or that learning a story verbatim is harder than learning the gist. By fifth grade, however, children can be rather articulate in explaining task differences. Kreutzer et al. (1975) reported the following interview of a fifth grader:

121

[Tester]: The other day I played a record of a story for a girl. I asked her to listen carefully to the record as many times as she wanted so she could tell me the story later. Before she began to listen to the record, she asked me one question: "Am I supposed to remember the story word for word, just like on the record, or can I tell you in my own words?" . . . Why do you think she asked this question? [P. 43]

[Child]: Because if it was word for word she would probably listen to it many times so she could memorize it. But if it was in her own words, she would not have to listen to it so much because she could get the idea, and then put it in her own words. [P. 49]

[Tester]: Would it be easier to learn it word for word, or in her own words? [P. 43]

[Child]: Be easier to learn it in her own words. You could like explain. But if you have to learn it word for word, you might forget some of the words, and that would ruin the whole story. But if you do it in your own words, you just try to get the main ideas, and then if you kind of get stuck, you could just fill it in. [P. 49]

[Tester]: If I told her to learn it word for word, what do you suppose she did? [P. 43]

[Child]: Croaked! Asked for it a second time—she can't take notes, can she? [No.] Well—she could remember it word for word and say it over again but that—how long was the story? If it's pretty long, *nobody* could remember it! [P. 49]

The final category of metamemory concerns what children know about the variety of *strategies* available to aid memory. Older children can think of more different ways to remind themselves, as the following excerpt from the Kreutzer et al. (1975) study shows.

[Tester]: Suppose you were going ice skating with your friend after school tomorrow and you wanted to be sure to bring your skates. How could you be really certain that you didn't forget to bring your skates along to school in the morning? [P. 25]

[Third grader]: I could put them in my book bag, or set them on the table. Or I could always write myself a note, and put it up on my bulletin board. Or I could tell my mom to remind me. Or I could take them to school the day before and just leave them there. [P. 29]

The topic of metamemory is too recent to allow a clear understanding of the relationship between it and actual memory performance. Preliminary research suggests two tentative conclusions. First, children who understand certain aspects of a memory task reflect that knowledge in their actual memory performance. Second, metamemory is less related to memory performance for younger children than for older children. That is, metamemory develops, memory performance improves, and the coordination between the two develops (Flavell & Wellman, 1977).

General world knowledge   Metamemory is one specific kind of knowledge which influences memory performance. In addition, memory is influenced by more general knowledge of the world, such as knowledge about language, people, places, objects, and events. Using this broader knowledge is the third "control process" which might explain developmental changes in memory performance. Younger children usually have less knowledge about most topics, and they usually remember less. (Recall that even six-year-olds know that greater familiarity with a topic enhances memory.) When children have more knowledge than adults (e.g., when comparing child chess experts to adult novices for memory of chessboard arrangements), the children remember more (Chi, 1978). Yet, even when children have some knowledge, they often fail to use it to aid their memories. In one study of this phenomenon, Paris and Lindauer (1976) read sentences to school-aged children involving a person engaged in an activity. An instrument or tool normally used in the activity was either stated explicitly or left unstated but implicit. For example, one implicit sentence was "The workman dug a hole in the ground." For the comparable explicit sentence, the phrase "with a shovel" was added. After hearing eight such sentences, the children were asked to recall all of the sentences. To aid their recall, all children were told the instruments (e.g., "the shovel") as cues. Six-year-olds recalled more sentences when the instrument had been explicitly stated than sentences when the instrument had merely been implied. Ten-year-olds recalled the explicit and implicit sentences equally well. If a child had drawn the necessary inference at the time of encoding the sentence (as the ten-year-olds did), the instrument served as a useful recall cue. Because the six-year-olds could not make use of the recall cues for the implicit sentences, we can conclude that they were not as likely to draw the inferences about the instruments when they first heard the sentences. Similar age differences have been found in other studies; younger children are less likely to infer pre-existing conditions or consequences of actions in a story (Paris & Upton, 1976).

Involuntary Memory

In contrast to the deliberate memory described above, in which memory is the goal, memory can also be involuntary or non-deliberate, arising as a by-product of other activities. Two lines of research have emphasized involuntary memory: the levels of processing approach and the Soviet approach.

Levels of processing approach   The levels of processing model of memory started from the assumption that cognitive analysis of a stimulus could occur at several levels, each of which would produce a memory trace as a by-product (Craik & Lockhart, 1972). For example, at a sensory level of analysis, the physical properties of a stimulus would be analyzed. If the stimulus was the word _sheep_, a sensory analysis would permit a person to decide that the word was five letters long or printed in lower case letters. At a semantic level of analysis, the meaning of the word would be analyzed, permitting a person to decide that the word *sheep* represented a farm animal.

Experimentally, the phenomenon was studied by giving subjects the encoding task of answering questions about words. Sometimes the questions required a sensory analysis, such as "Is the next word printed in capital letters? BOOK," and the subject would respond "yes" or "no." Other questions, such as "Does the next word rhyme with hook? BOOK," evoked the intermediate level of phonemic analysis. Some questions required a semantic analysis, for example, "Is the next word something you can read? BOOK." Later, subjects were unexpectedly asked to recall or recognize all the words that they had seen. Typically for adults, semantically encoded words were remembered more than the sensory- and rhyme-encoded words.

Initially, the levels of processing theory proposed that the sensory analysis was a shallow processing which occurred before the deeper semantic analysis. Now the theory proposes . that the different levels of analysis are qualitatively different and give rise to qualitatively different memory traces, but their time sequence is not predetermined (Craik, 1979). Under some circumstances, sensory encoding can produce better memory than semantic encoding (Kolers, 1979), so "depth" of processing is now defined in terms of the amount of attention and effort required to answer the encoding questions (Jacoby & Craik, 1979). Factors which influence the depth of encoding in the levels of processing model are analogous to those influencing the control processes in the multistore model (Naus, Ornstein, & Hoving, 1978). For example, more elaborated semantic processing enhances memory, whether it is forced through an involuntary orienting procedure or deliberately initiated by the memorizer.

In applying the levels of processing approach to the development of memory in children, three questions have been asked. The answers, however, are only tentative because very few studies have been done. The questions are as follows:

1. Do children, like adults, show the same pattern of better

memory following semantic encoding compared with sensory or phonemic encoding? Apparently the answer is "yes" (Owings & Baumeister, 1979; Sophian & Hagen, 1978), at least for adolescents down to four-year-olds (the youngest children tested so far).

2. Assuming that older children are more skilled at semantic analysis than younger ones (they have more semantic knowledge), do older children show a better involuntary memory? Although this question is easy to pose, the answer is difficult to obtain because of two major methodological problems which plague experiments. First, no age differences will appear if the task is so easy that even the youngest children do very well (a ceiling effect) or so hard that even the oldest children do very poorly (a floor effect). Several of the studies using a levels of processing task with children have had these problems (e.g., Geis & Hall, 1976; Sophian & Hagen, 1978). Second, although deliberate memory encoding strategies are presumably not operating because the subjects do not even know that they are in a memory study, deliberate retrieval strategies cannot be avoided; the experimenter has to ask the children to try to remember the stimulus words. Any age differences found in an experiment could be attributed to the better use of retrieval strategies by older children instead of to a better initial encoding analysis. The best that can be done is to compare across ages in the different kinds of retrieval situations, that is, to compare memory performance under recognition, free recall, and cued recall. A large-scale study of this kind has not yet been done, but when results from several studies are pieced together, a consistent age pattern is not suggested (Geis & Hall, 1978; Mitchell & Ault, 1980; Owings & Baumeister, 1979; Sophian & Hagen, 1978). Some researchers have already concluded that involuntary memory is very good in young children and therefore does not improve much with age (Naus & Halasz, 1979). Retrieval strategies almost certainly confound the results, though, because cued recall is generally better than free recall (e.g., Mitchell & Ault, 1980).

3. The third question that can be asked about involuntary memory is how it compares to deliberate memory. Both American and Soviet research have found that children given a "favorable orienting task" (i.e., one that evokes deep processing) remember more than children trying to memorize deliberately but without any experimenter-supplied aids as to what strategies to use (Brown, 1979; Meacham, 1977). Because younger children have fewer and poorer deliberate strategies, the gap between involuntary and voluntary memory is greater for younger children and reduces with age.

Soviet approach   Soviet researchers have concluded that involuntary memory develops before voluntary memory. They observed that the natural activities of infants and preschoolers led the children into learning some cognitive skills, such as how to label and classify objects. Only after these skills were well developed as goals in their own right could children apply them as means to some other goal, in particular, as encoding strategies in a deliberate memory task. For instance, children usually name objects during play. When this skill is well practiced in that context, it transfers to other situations, such as naming objects when an experimenter presents them during a memory test. This naming is a primitive rehearsal strategy which later changes into repeating the series of object names. (Refer to Table 3-1 for examples of rehearsal sets.) Similarly, classifying objects into categories affords practice of an organizing strategy, but it first occurs in the context of play as its own goal. Then it transfers to deliberate memory situations. During the practice of these cognitive skills, involuntary memory arises as a by-product, so it develops before voluntary memory (Meacham, 1977; Smirnov & Zinchenko, 1969).

The above description of memory development illustrates three themes which underlie Soviet research and writing: (a) what is remembered is determined by an interaction between the material to be remembered and the child's activities with that material; (b) the child's activities, in turn, are determined

127

by social, historical, and cultural forces; and (c) activities change qualitatively with age and are marked more by change than by periods of stability and balance, that is, a dialectical model is advanced (Meacham, 1977; Vendovitskaya, 1971; Zaporozhets & Elkonin, 1971).

The first theme refers, for example, to having objects which can be named or sorted and a child trying to label or categorize them as opposed, say, to having a random collection of hard-to-name objects and a child who is interested in throwing the objects. The point can also be illustrated with a study by Leont'ev and Rozanova (as reported in Smirnov & Zinchenko, 1969). They presented children with a board containing 16 circles with a familiar word written on each circle. One at a time, in succession, each circle lit up. Children in one group were told to find the most frequent initial letter for the words and to remove those circles when they lit up. Children in a second group were told to remove each circle when it lit up if its word began with the letter s. Children in the third group were told whether or not to remove each circle as it lit up, with no explanation for the experimenter's choices. All children, in fact, removed exactly the same circles in the same order. Then the children were tested for their involuntary memory of the words and the initial letters on the circles.

The children's activities had a direct influence on what was remembered. In the first group, the children remembered all the different initial letters. In the second group, they remembered only the letter s. In the third group, none of the initial letters were remembered. As expected, none of the activities produced recall of the words because none of the activities required processing of the whole word.

The second Soviet theme, concerning sociohistorical and cultural influences, refers primarily to adult socialization pressures on children. Vendovitskaya (1971) wrote that recognition memory in infants seven to eight months old "is expressed initially by visual fixation on an object named by the adult and its shifting from object to object [depends] on [adult] verbal designation" (p. 91). Adults encourage children to name objects, and they point out what should be remembered, prompt how to do so, and reinforce the child's efforts. Children develop deliberate memory in part because of adult demands to do so.

The third theme stresses changes in children's activities. In infancy, the dominant characteristic activity is manipulating objects (equivalent to Piaget's Sensorimotor schemes). In the preschool years, the dominant activity is playing games, especially imaginary ones. In the elementary school years, school tasks set by teachers and other adults are dominant, and in adolescence, intimate personal relations and career-related activities are dominant (Meacham, 1977; Zaporozhets & Elkonin, 1971).

We have seen how the naming and sorting activities of early childhood promote the development of mnemonic skills which will later be used in deliberate memory situations. In addition, the play of preschoolers gives contextual support for early deliberate memory attempts. For example, in building a toy boat, children might need to get several items off a shelf. To remember the items, the children might deliberately rehearse as they walk across the room to the shelf. This kind of practice, supported by the context of play, later enables children to use rehearsal out of any context, for example, in school, to learn a list of vocabulary words by rote (Brown, 1979).

The memory studies done by the Soviet psychologists have provided impetus for American researchers to use more naturalistic situations to study memory and to pay more attention to involuntary memory. While new discoveries are sure to be made, the distinction between deliberate and involuntary memory is primarily restricted to the encoding phase, and some researchers (e.g., Hagen, 1979) do not believe the distinction is all that clear. No matter how information gets into memory, the storage and retrieval phases do not seem to differ with encoding method (or, at least, no one has yet proposed such a distinction). With information in memory and retrievable from it, the child is ready to use perception and memory to generate and test hypotheses in the final process of thought.

GENERATION AND TESTING OF HYPOTHESES

After children recognize that a problem must be solved, they must generate a set of hypotheses (possible solutions). The size of this set and the adequacy (appropriateness) of the hypotheses depend on children's prior experiences with similar problems. If children have had many prior experiences, they can often generalize quite easily from the old problems to the new ones. Thus, older children will, in general, be better able to solve a new problem merely because they have had more experience with similar problems on which to base their hypotheses. Children with a wider variety of cognitive units (schemata, symbols, concepts, and rules) are more likely to find a solution because they can draw on more knowledge. After children think of a hypothesis (the generation phase), they must acquire information to confirm or disconfirm it (the testing phase).

Let us compare four hypothetical children, ages 3, 4, 5, and 6 years, to demonstrate hypothesis generation and testing. Each child is taken into a room and is told that when he comes out, he can play with a toy. The experimenter then leaves the room, shutting the door afterward. Each child immediately goes to the door to try to open it. The three-year-old has learned one rule about doors: they can be pushed or pulled. On the basis of this one rule, he generates two hypotheses. One is that the door should be pushed; the other is that the door should be pulled. The child tests these two hypotheses by pushing and pulling the door, but it does not open. The four-year-old has learned the same rule about pushing and pulling, but because he has had more experience with doors, he has learned a second rule: doorknobs can be turned clockwise or counterclockwise. The four-year-old tests various hypotheses by combinations of pushing, pulling, and turning the doorknob. Eventually, he finds that he should first turn the knob clockwise and then pull the door. The five-year-old has more elaborate rules about opening doors. He knows, for example, that doorknobs almost always turn clockwise and that they must be turned before pushing or pulling. His problem is very much simpler than the three-year-old's and also easier than the four-year-old's because he has more exact rules. He only needs to generate and test the hypothesis about pushing vs. pulling. A still older child, say six years old, might have watched the experimenter leave the room and observed whether the door swung inward or outward. He could then open the door the very first time he tried because the hypothesis he would generate to test first would be completely appropriate.

To get out of the room, the child had to generate hypotheses about how doors open. When the hypotheses are insufficient, as in the case of the three-year-old, the child may never solve the problem.* If the hypotheses are more or less adequate but must be combined in novel ways, as in the cases of the four- and five-year-olds, we can observe complex hypothesis testing. When prior learning is sufficient, as in the case of the six-year-old, only one hypothesis needs to be generated, and it is likely to be the correct solution. As the child accumulates experience, the expectation of correctness increases until the hypothesis is considered to be a rule. If such a hypothesis turns out to be incorrect, perhaps due to an external agent like Candid Camera or a devious experimenter, considerable consternation can result.

The example above serves as a good practical illustration of hypothesis generation and hypothesis testing. Natural situations, however, usually contain uncontrollable aspects, such as the exact kind of experience with doors each child has had. Researchers generally turn to artificial problems which offer greater control of unwanted variations in exchange for some lack of naturalness. We shall now describe a few experimental studies of the generation and testing of hypotheses to illustrate

* Of course, he may generate and test one further hypothesis, that if he screams loudly enough, someone is likely to let him out.

131

the developmental changes in this process of thought. Such experiments can be divided into two categories. One is based on the child's verbal statements; the other analyzes a sequence of nonverbal behaviors.

A verbal technique—Twenty Questions

Under the topic of a concept's accessibility, we described the Twenty Questions game. Children are shown an array of pictures (refer to Figures 3-2 and 3-3) and told to guess which one the experimenter has in mind by asking questions that can be answered by "yes" or "no." The questions which children ask have been classified into four types. One kind of question has been labeled a *specific hypothesis*. The child names one of the pictures and asks specifically about it. Examples are "Is it the kite?" and "Is it the monkey?" The specific hypothesis is obviously the least efficient question that could be asked because only one picture can be eliminated from the array with each query. A general question which can eliminate more than one alternative, on the other hand, is a *constraint-seeking question*. Children can fashion constraint-seeking questions along many different conceptual dimensions. Questions can refer to some perceptual feature of the objects such as their color, size, shape, or distinctive markings. Examples of such perceptual constraint-seeking questions are "Is it yellow?" and "Does it have a tail?" Other types of constraint-seeking questions may refer to an object's function ("Can you eat it?"), classification ("Is it an animal?"), location in the array ("Is it in the first row?"), and so forth. For the sake of simplicity, these constraint-seeking questions are designated nonperceptual. Finally, it is useful to distinguish an intermediate type called *pseudocon-straint-seeking questions*. These questions appear to have the form of a true constraint-seeking question but, like a specific hypothesis, they refer to only one picture. Examples are "Is it like a horse but with black and white stripes?" (the zebra) and "Is it green with a flower on it?" (the sprinkling can).

132

The sequence for the types of questions that children of various ages will generate is well established. As you might suspect, specific hypotheses are the predominant type of question for children under the age of six or seven years. When children learn that guessing specific pictures is "wrong," they try to use the more advanced types, but at first only the *form* of the question is learned. Pseudoconstraint-seeking questions, therefore, play a transitional role between specific hypotheses and constraint-seeking questions. Of the two major types of constraint-seeking questions, perceptual ones appear first, perhaps because perceptual *concepts* are more accessible to younger children. As children gain experience dealing with nonperceptual categories, they use nonperceptual constraint-seeking questions more. Whether perceptual questions are as efficient as nonperceptual questions depends on the particular set of pictures used in the game. In general, however, the non-perceptual questions will be more efficient, and this fact probably explains why children come to prefer them (Ault, 1973; Mosher & Hornsby, 1966).

The Twenty Questions game is one way of measuring change in children's hypothesis generation, but it has two drawbacks. It is dependent to some extent on children's verbal skills, and it does not discriminate among children below the age of 6 to 7, or above the age of 11 to 12 years. In other words, its range of applicability is restricted. Because it is unreasonable to suppose that no differences exist in hypothesis generation between a 3-year-old and a 6-year-old, or between a 12-year-old and a college student, researchers have used nonverbal tasks which permit a wider age range to be studied.

A nonverbal technique—probability learning

The most common probability learning task presents the subject with three buttons on a panel and some method of delivering a reward, such as a hole through which marbles can be dropped. The subject is instructed to push one button at a

133

time. If the correct button is pushed, a marble comes out. The goal is to get as many marbles as possible in a fixed number of trials (button pushes). Two of the three buttons are never correct and hence never result in marbles. The third button is partially correct. Some fraction of the time, say 33 percent, subjects get a marble if they push this button. For the other 67 percent of the time, they get nothing after pushing it. Obviously, subjects cannot obtain a marble on every trial. The best they can do is push the "correct" button all the time and get marbles after a third of these pushes. This strategy is called *maximizing* because subjects maximize their chances of getting marbles. If they push either of the other two buttons, they get fewer marbles.

Weir (1964) compiled data for 80 trials on subjects ranging in age from 3 to 19 years. The 3-year-olds adopt the maximizing strategy fairly soon after the experiment begins, and by the last block of 20 trials, they push the correct button as much as 80 percent of the time. The 19-year-olds also maximize by the last 20 trials, but they take many more trials to reach this point. At the intermediate ages, from 5 to 15 years, children push the correct button less than 50 percent of the time, even after 80 trials. This finding is surprising since 3-year-olds rarely perform better on any task than school age children or arrive at the solution (maximizing) faster than college students. To explain these startling results, we need to examine the sequence of button-pushing which children exhibit across all the trials.

The 3-year-olds spend a few trials trying all the different buttons. Then they seem to settle on the correct button and push it most of the time. The 5- to 9-year-olds tend to adopt some alternating patterns, such as left-middle-right or right-middle-left, which yield few marbles, and the 11- to 15-year-olds sometimes formulate even more complex alternations. Why do these children persist in testing elaborate patterns when the success rate for them is so low? There are many potential reasons, but two major ones are (a) the expectation which children bring to the experiment and (b) the skill which the children have for generating and testing hypotheses. If children come to the task expecting a higher rate of success than is actually available, they will look for solutions which match their expectations. In other words, they will continue to generate patterns of responses in hopes that one of these patterns will "pay off" at the expected rate, even though searching for this pattern costs them marbles. In contrast, the 3-year-olds do not seem to expect to get marbles on every trial, perhaps because they do not consider themselves very successful on such tasks. They willingly settle for marbles on only 33 percent of the trials. Older children who have expectations of finding completely correct solutions (i.e., getting marbles after every trial) continue to generate and test hypotheses, looking for a pattern of responses which they believe will earn them more marbles (Stevenson, 1972).

In addition, 3-year-olds may not generate very many hypotheses about how to push the buttons. They try each button in turn, discover that two never pay off, and so settle on the third button. Children of intermediate ages generate many elaborate hypotheses, but their ability to test these patterns is not fully developed. Their memory may not be sufficient to remember exactly which sequences have been tried and which remain to be tried. They may not organize the potential sequences in a logical way (which would help them remember where they are in their search). Moreover, they probably consider each sequence equally likely. Older subjects, such as the 19-year-olds, might decide that the experimenter is unlikely to choose highly idiosyncratic patterns, so such patterns are rejected without being tested. Older children can also organize their search in a more efficient and logical manner, and they can keep better track of where they are. Thus, many college students eventually test the hypothesis that one button is paying off at a less-than-perfect rate, and they settle for this.

In the probability learning situation, subjects have virtually unlimited numbers of hypotheses they can generate, and they must also devise some system for testing all of the hypotheses in the number of trials allowed. Hypothesis generation and hypothesis testing cannot be controlled or observed separately in the probability learning task. In order to see the influence of hypothesis testing alone, a different nonverbal task should be used. In it, subjects are given a limited set of hypotheses to choose from so that hypothesis generation is not a factor.

Levine's blank trials procedure

Tasks called *cue-selection problems* have long been used to assess adult hypothesis testing. The basic task presents subjects with a set of dimensions (e.g., shape, color, size), each of which is represented by several values. The four stimulus pairs in Figure 3-13 show four dimensions (and two values) as follows: letter (*x* or *t*), size (*large* or *small*), color (*black* or *white*), and bar location (*over* or *under*).* Subjects are asked to determine which value of one of the dimensions is correct. Since the different possible values are clearly specified, hypothesis generation is not a factor; the burden falls on hypothesis testing.

Levine (1966) developed a procedure to assess which hypothesis a subject tested in the cue-selection problem. If subjects tested the same hypothesis for each of the four pairs in Figure 3-13, they would exhibit a unique pattern of left and right choices. For example, if the hypothesis is that *t* is correct, a right-left-left-left pattern will be shown. If the hypothesis is that *white* is correct, the pattern will be right-left-right-right. In all, subjects can exhibit eight unique patterns corresponding to the eight stimulus values, each of which will have three responses to one side and one response to the other.

In another study, Levine and his colleagues showed that subjects would continue with one hypothesis if they received no feedback on that trial about whether they were correct or incorrect (Levine, Leitenberg, & Richter, 1964). If subjects could

---

* Early versions of this task used left or right position of the stimulus as the fourth dimension, but that allowed young children who show a position preference to appear to be testing hypotheses (see Gholson, 1980).

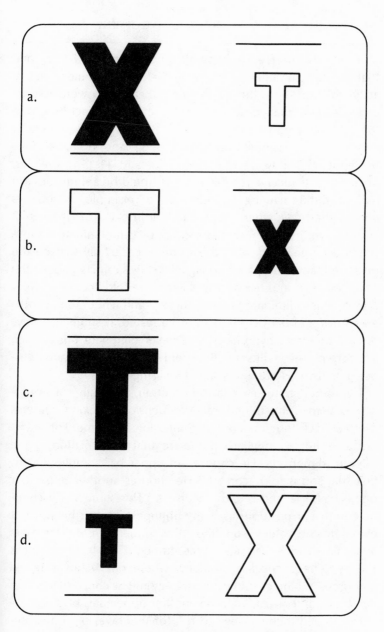

Figure 3-13. Four stimulus pairs used in hypothesis testing

be given four no-feedback (or blank) trials in a row (e.g., one trial on each stimulus pair of Figure 3-13), one could infer exactly which of the eight possible hypotheses they were testing. Levine's blank trials procedure incorporated this fact by giving the subjects feedback only every fifth trial. Subjects are told "correct" or "incorrect" on trials 1, 6, 11, and 16 and receive no feedback following trials 2-5, 7-10, and 11-15. Moreover, once subjects receive feedback, they should be able to discard half of the remaining hypotheses. For example, if subjects choose the *small, white, t,* and *bar over* in pair a of Figure 3-13 and receive the feedback "correct," they can eliminate the hypotheses *large, black, x,* and *bar under.* Let us say that on the next feedback trial (pair b of Figure 3-13), subjects choose the *small, black, x,* and *bar over* and again are told "correct." Now they can also eliminate the hypotheses *t* and *white;* the hypotheses *small* and *bar over* remain to be tested. If subjects always discard incorrect hypotheses and never eliminate ones which are correct, they will solve the problem in the minimum number of trials. This strategy is called *focusing.*

Two other strategies lead to a solution, although not as efficiently as focusing. In one, called *dimension checking,* subjects use feedback to eliminate one dimension at a time. For example, one subject might hypothesize that bar position is the relevant dimension. He chooses an upper bar stimulus on his first trial and is told "correct." He chooses another upper bar on his next trial and is told "incorrect." This subject will eliminate both bar positions as being unimportant, but he will not eliminate the values from the other dimensions (letter, size, and color) which were also disconfirmed. Even less efficient is the *hypothesis checking* strategy, where one value is tested at a time. A subject using this strategy might choose an upper bar, be told "correct," choose another upper bar, be told "incorrect," and then proceed to test for the lower bar on subsequent trials.

Some subjects exhibit stereotyped response sequences which are rule-governed but do not lead to a solution because feedback does not alter the rule. In the *position perseveration* stereotype, a subject will choose whatever stimulus is on the left (or right) and be correct only part of the time. A *position alternation* stereotype is shown by a simple left-right-left-right sequence, again maintained despite feedback. For the *stimulus preference* stereotype, subjects continually pick one of the four stimulus values but never drop the hypothesis when told it is incorrect.

Gholson and Beilin (1979) summarized the general developmental trends found for hypothesis testing as follows: kindergarten children (about $5\frac{1}{2}$ years old) show stereotypes in 90 percent of the problems. Elementary school children (7 to 12 years old) show hypothesis checking and dimension checking 65 to 80 percent of the time and focusing 5 to 15 percent. College students focus at least 50 percent and never show stereotypes.

Rules can also be inferred on other problems, such as conservation of number or Piaget's Formal Operational tasks. Siegler (1978) tested children as young as 3 and 4 years old and reported that 4-year-olds used rules only sometimes and 3-year-olds "almost never conform to any easily describable formula" (p. 131). When asked to explain how they decided what stimulus to choose, 3-year-olds reply, "I chose the one that was special" and "I chose the one I wanted to" (p. 131). Before concluding that 3-year-olds simply do not use rules, Siegler (1981) noted that one should consider the possibilities that the children use rules on some trials but not consistently enough to be detected and that they try to use rules but fail to execute their plans accurately. In any case, it is clear that rule-governed hypothesis testing increases steadily throughout childhood.

INTERRELATIONS

One might suppose that the processes of thought operate in the same sequence as they have been presented here: perception, memory, and hypothesis generation and testing—a sequence that follows an intuitively logical order. However, it is possible that the processes do not operate sequentially. *Parallel* (or simultaneous) processing is an attractive explanation of why thinking can occur so rapidly, and current theories from the fields of information processing and computer science argue for parallel processing systems.

The interrelationship of the development of the units of thought and the development of the processes of thought is not precisely known, but it is reasonable to assume that their changes correspond over time. The functioning of each process affects the development of each unit of thought. Perception, for example, must play a central role in the development of symbols and concepts. Since symbols are arbitrary expressions for schemata, the schemata have to be refined by the perceptual process before symbols can be assigned to them. All of the units of thought are stored in and retrieved from memory; therefore, any limitation of the memory process will necessarily limit the development of the units. The units cannot be enriched, differentiated, made more precise, or validated until the old unit is recalled from memory and the new one replaces it. In a similar manner, as children generate and test various hypotheses about the meaning of certain concepts, those concepts might change in status or validity. While it might appear that fairly clear distinctions have been made between each of the units and processes, this appearance is deceptive. Instead of being discrete, the units and processes are interwoven, and it is difficult to draw fine lines between them.

In addition to the units and processes of thought, several other factors influence the likelihood that children will solve a problem. Among these factors are cultural conditioning, anxiety (e.g., fear of failure), motivation (e.g., desire to succeed, avoid errors, or to obtain a reward), and expectations for success or failure. All of these variables become more salient with age, but whether they facilitate or impede problem solving depends on the particular individual. Since these factors are neither general developmental variables nor, strictly speaking, units or processes of thought, we shall not elaborate on them.

SUMMARY

The process approach to cognitive development identifies four units and three processes of thought. Developmentally, children shift from primary reliance on schemata to the greater use of symbols, concepts, and rules. Quantitative increases occur in the number of units a child has, and the units themselves change in ways which are usually described as quantitative. For example, concepts gain validity, status, and accessibility and come to be used relatively as well as absolutely. Children gradually prefer formal and transformational rules to informal and nontransformational ones, but all remain available.

Among the more interesting changes in the development of the perceptual process are increases in children's attention span, better selectivity of attention, greater speed in shifting attention, and more rapid and more accurate final perceptions. Performance on deliberate memory tasks also increases dramatically during childhood. The multistore model suggests that most of this increase can be attributed to the control aspects (strategies, particularly organization; metamemory; and general world knowledge). It is not yet clear how much change occurs in involuntary memory. When tested in an involuntary memory situation or with recognition as the mode of retrieval, young children appear to have fairly good memories, especially in contrast to their deliberate memory performance or when recall, rather than recognition, is the retrieval mode. The third process of thought, generation and testing of hypotheses, also undergoes change with age. As children develop, they generate more adequate and sophisticated hypotheses and then test these hypotheses more systematically and efficiently. Tasks such as Twenty Questions, probability learning, and Levine's blank trials procedure for the cue-selection problem demonstrate the generation and testing of hypotheses in both verbal and nonverbal situations.

141

4

A COMPARISON OF APPROACHES

Some similarities and differences between Piaget's approach and the process approach have already been explored, but because they have been embedded in other contexts, they have probably not been highly salient. Therefore, the purpose of this brief chapter is to make the previous comparisons more prominent and to add some new ones. We start with a look at the interactionist and active child assumptions common to both approaches. We then examine how each approach supports the moderate novelty principle and how they differ in their stances on the nature and rate of developmental change (stage vs. nonstage theory). Then we contrast Piaget's views of perception, memory, and hypothesis testing with the process approach.

SIMILARITIES IN ASSUMPTIONS

Most cognitive psychologists consider themselves interactionists (rather than nativists or empiricists), in part because the extreme maturation and learning stances seem untenable. As Kumler (1971) expressed it:

Imagine that you are listening to a drummer beating on a drum. Nobody would try to figure out which noises were produced by the drum and which noises were produced by the drummer. . . . Every trait results entirely from an interaction of the innate composition of the organism and the experience. [P. 184]

Neither Piagetian nor process approach researchers have spent time trying to estimate how much of some problem-solving behavior is due to heredity or the environment. While it may seem strange to say that two approaches are similar for what they do *not* do, they both stand in contrast to the third major approach to studying intelligence—the standardized IQ testing movement—which has recently been the context for a raging heredity-vs.-environment controversy (see Jensen, 1969, 1977; Scarr-Salapatek, 1971; Scarr & Weinberg, 1976). Piaget's explicit introduction of concepts grounded in biology (e.g., assimilation and accommodation) and his advocacy of a stage theory helped earn him the reputation of being a maturationist, yet he clearly subscribed to the interactionist position. The biological factors were not merely fixed bases on which the environment built its modifications. Nor were stages preformed, waiting to unfold in time. Rather, Piaget intertwined the biological and environmental factors, saying that each affected the functioning of the other. One example is that assimilation and accommodation are influenced by particular experiences, such as imaginative play or imitation. On the other hand, the child's current developmental status influences the interpretation and storing of stimulus events. The enrichment theory in perception and the constructivist approaches to memory (e.g., Paris & Lindauer, 1977) agree with Piaget on these points. Process approach researchers are, however, more likely to consider a biological base as innately given and to emphasize experiential factors (Beilin, 1981). The differentiation theory of perception, for example, focuses on what distinctive features are inherent in a stimulus. This puts process approach researchers toward the

143

environmental side of the continuum, but they are still inter-actionists.

The second common assumption, as described in Chapter 1, was that children are active rather than passive participants in their own development. Perhaps a more accurate and less simplistic way to state this assumption is to say that certain aspects of development begin relatively passively and become decidedly more active. The behavior patterns of very young infants in Piaget's first stage of the Sensorimotor Period are essentially passive. Infants cannot, for example, avoid practicing their reflexes and schemes whenever an appropriate stimulus is presented. They are, at first, bound to suck on their thumbs or grasp a rattle. Within a very short time, however, these reflexes give way to more voluntary behaviors. But for Piaget, children are active in a more important sense: they actively construct their own knowledge structures. Knowledge is not poured into an empty brain nor absorbed as a blotter draws up ink. Knowledge is built out of children's actions on their environment. Even though a bottle may be placed in a newborn's mouth, triggering sucking, knowing the bottle as something to be sucked results from both the bottle's physical characteristics and the child's participation. The active child assumption means that characteristics of the child are as important, if not more so, than environmental stimulus characteristics.

The process approach also describes a trend from passivity to active control, especially in the areas of attention and memory. Early attention is said to be "captured" by certain stimulus features such as high contrast and movement, which automatically provoke attention. As Neisser (1979) said, "It does 'force itself' on the perceiver . . . because she cannot help being prepared for it" (p. 213). Nevertheless, attention becomes more volitional and selective; it comes under the active control of the perceiver. As children develop, they show increasing ability to ignore irrelevant material and to distribute their attention according to the task's demands.

In memory, the passive-to-active trend is most obvious in

the shift from involuntary to deliberate memory. As its very name suggests, involuntary memory is not fully controlled by the memorizer. Certain encodings occur automatically; one cannot avoid storing some aspects of an experience. As we saw with the Stroop effect in which the names of colors were printed in different colored letters, the name spelled by the word is a powerful stimulus and only older subjects are able to exert enough control to prevent processing the word's name (Lockhart, Craik, & Jacoby, 1976). In retrieval too, some experiences are recognized as familiar without any active attempt to retrieve the old experience. Infants are fairly capable of this relatively passive memory. With development, however, children become skilled in the more active, deliberate memory. Strategies, such as organization and rehearsal, give the memorizer the ability to select what will be memorized and when and how it will be retrieved.

The moderate novelty principle is a third common ground between the two approaches. In Piaget's terminology, moderately discrepant events allow both assimilation and accommodation, and so yield the most change in knowledge. If an event is moderately different from previous ones, children will have old structures (schemes and operations) which can be applied (i.e., assimilated), but the structures will be modified because the new event has some novel features which must be accommodated. If an event is too familiar, children will only assimilate it. If it is too novel, children will not be able to modify old structures enough to fit the new event, so no accommodation will occur. Thus moderately novel or discrepant events are preferred.

In the process approach terminology, moderately discrepant events yield maximum attention. Events which are too familiar lead to rapid habituation. Events which are too novel do not contain enough accessible information to be meaningful. In terms of enrichment theory, no old schemata will be appropriate to be added. In terms of differentiation theory, the distinctive features of the novel stimulus will not be recognized.

Both theories agree that a certain amount of redundancy in information is required, especially by young children, to make sense of perceptual input.

DIFFERENCES IN EMPHASIS

Despite the similarities in assumptions, Piaget's approach and the process approach differ in some fundamental regards. Most striking is the characterization of developmental change as stagelike or nonstagelike. As was discussed in Chapter 2, Piaget believed that the interesting developmental changes were the qualitative ones which separated the four major periods. Concrete Operations, for instance, are not just more refined Preoperational mental representations. A new feature (reversibility) is added which makes Concrete Operational thinking different in kind from Preoperational thinking. Moreover, Piaget's stage theory contains an ideal end state (Formal Operations) toward which children inevitably progress (see Figure 4-1). As long as development continues, its direction is specified.

Most of the research which characterizes the process approach emphasizes the quantitative nature of developmental change. Perceptions become more efficient, more distinctive features are identified, more strategies are available for encoding and retrieving memories, more hypotheses can be generated and tested more systematically, and so forth. Stages do not seem appropriate to this conceptualization. Moreover, the end goal of development is less well specified in the process approach.

By virtue of being a stage theory, Piaget's theory takes two positions regarding developmental sequences. (a) A fixed sequence should occur for the acquisition of a concept. That is, the partial understandings of a concept like conservation should form a fixed series leading to the full mastery of the concept. (b) Within each major period, different concepts should occur simultaneously. Recall that these were the invari-

Figure 4-1. An ideal end state in stage theory. Piaget's "stages" of cognitive development pictured as the stages used to launch a spacecraft: (bottom to top) the Sensorimotor and Preoperational stages are jettisoned as the Concrete Operational child follows a trajectory toward the Formal Operational goal.

ant sequence and cognitive structure (or concurrence) criteria discussed in Chapter 2 under the topic of stage theory.

Because the process approach is not, in fact, as unified an approach as Piaget's, it is harder to identify a particular stance on the issues of developmental sequences. In general, process approach researchers are more likely to agree with point (a) that some conceptual development is marked by fixed sequences than with point (b) that major concepts develop simultaneously. A fixed sequence was identified for the development of attention to perceptual features, from edges to angles to simple forms, and so on. Memory researchers found that some strategies develop in a regular pattern (e.g., in rehearsal, repeating each item in isolation precedes repeating mixed groups of items). In hypothesis testing, a regular sequence of rule usage could be seen in the Twenty Questions game and Levine's blank trials procedure. To the extent that process approach researchers do not hypothesize any superordinate cognitive structures, they have no reason to predict concurrent development between concepts. As we saw in Chapter 2, the presence of *decalages* on Piagetian tasks is a serious stumbling block to Piaget's version of a stage theory. From the process approach perspective, Siegler (1981) proposed a much more complex picture of developmental sequences across concepts. When children are unfamiliar with a particular problem, they may tackle it by using one simple strategy or rule. As they gain experiences with some problems compared with others, they make irregular advances but they do *not* transfer their advances across problems because they lack critical pieces of information that would make such transfers successful. Therefore, development appears more synchronous at younger ages and less so at older ages.

Critics of the process approach continue to believe in the existence of overarching mental structures.

> It is . . . structure that gives the rules meaning, and without meaning the rules seem somewhat vacuous. . . . We should

> look for higher-order organizations that can predict which
> kinds of rules will emerge at different age levels as children
> cope with various tasks. [Strauss & Levin, 1981, pp. 79-80]

Critics of Piaget's stage theory counter that

> wide variation in the age of mastery of concepts that are
> theoretically within the same stage has been the rule rather
> than the exception. This has led to the serious question of
> whether there is any generality in the way that children of
> particular ages approach different problems and to the rather
> unsettling possibility that there might be none. [Siegler,
> 1981, p. 2]

Obviously, debate will continue for some time on this issue.

SIMILARITIES IN TOPICS

Because both Piagetian and process approach researchers investigate cognitive development, it should not be surprising
that the topics each studies overlap considerably. In the following comparisons, the process organization is adopted because
it was easier to bend Piaget's work to focus on processes than
the reverse. Whereas Piaget has incorporated each process into
his description of stages, the process approach has, until recently, ignored Piaget's stages, classifying children solely by
ages. Since age does not predict very accurately what stage a
child might be in, it is more difficult to fit the process approach
to Piaget's theory. The organization of the next few pages is not
intended to convey approval of one approach over the other;
it is merely a statement of the relative ease of presentation.

PERCEPTION

Piaget has suggested a theory of perception, but it is less complete and less accessible to readers than his theory of cognitive

development. Gibson (1969) has classified Piaget's theory of perception as an enrichment theory because information from schemata are added to the basic sensory data through the process of assimilation and the schemata, in turn, are modified to accommodate the specific stimulus input. The characterization of Piaget's theory as an enrichment theory focuses attention on the schemata that become enriched. Piaget's theory has an additional focus, however, on the development of certain mental operations, similar to cognitive operations, that influence perception (Elkind, 1975). Those operations are *perceptual regulations* which give children new methods of manipulating perceptual data mentally. At first, children's perceptions are centered on a few aspects of the stimulus which are highly salient and which capture their attention. The stimulus controls attention, so attention is stimulus-bound (just as it is in the process approach). According to Piaget, the development of perceptual regulations frees children's attention, allowing them to choose and control where they direct their attention. In other words, perception becomes decentered through the operation of perceptual regulations. The change from centering to decentering is directly analogous to the improvements in selective attention discussed under the process approach.

To make these ideas clearer, we can consider two abilities that arise from the development of perceptual regulations. One of them involves mentally rearranging a stimulus event by combining or separating various aspects of it to create a new perception. Some visual stimuli, for example, can be viewed as two different figures, depending on which areas are seen as central to a figure and which as the background. The young child centers on only one organization and perceives a single figure. The older child is able to decenter and reorganize the stimulus to perceive both figures. Piaget attributed the ability to reorganize the picture to perceptual regulations which allow children to add or subtract areas and contours from the picture to form all the possible figures and their corresponding backgrounds. The picture in Figure 4-2 is perceived as a vase if the

150

Figure 4-2. An ambiguous figure with two perceptual organizations

black area is considered the central figure and the white area (the entire image minus the black area) is the background. The picture is perceived as two faces if the white area is the central figure and the black area is the background.

The other perceptual ability involves part–whole perception. To test this, children are shown a set of pictures in which one familiar object is constructed using other familiar objects as parts. For instance, a man can be made up of pieces of fruit, with bananas representing his legs and a pear representing his body. Children who have not yet acquired the necessary per-

151

ceptual regulations will center only on the parts and report seeing the fruit, or they will center only on the whole and report seeing the man. Children who have the perceptual regulations, however, can decenter and see both the parts and the whole simultaneously, reporting a man made up of fruit. These perceptual regulations are analogous to the cognitive operations used in the part—whole (class inclusion) task. According to Piaget, in both tasks, children must consider simultaneously more than one facet of the problem or stimulus.

MEMORY

Piaget's work on memory focuses on the ways memories are influenced by general world knowledge. Thus it is compatible with the section of the multistore model concerned with general world knowledge and with the levels of processing approach. Specifically, Piaget and Inhelder (1973) suggested that the accuracy of memories should be related to children's stages of cognitive development. The levels of processing approach also "views memory as the assimilation of incoming information into one's current knowledge base [so that] a child's existing semantic knowledge determines . . . what is remembered" (Naus et al., 1978, pp. 227-28). Both positions suggest that memory performance can actually improve with time, whereas most memory theories merely try to explain memory deterioration. The levels of processing model emphasizes that the match between the encoding and retrieval environments (Tulving & Thomson, 1973) might be better on a delayed recall attempt compared with an earlier one. Piaget and Inhelder, on the other hand, stressed changes in the actual memory representation (what is stored). Memories can become more accurate over time if children acquire new operations which pertain to the memory representation.

Three types of evidence have been sought to evaluate the position of Piaget and Inhelder. The weakest evidence merely shows that memory performance improves with age (as does cognitive operational level). Piaget and Inhelder (1973), for example, showed three- to eight-year-old children a set of sticks arranged in order by size (the seriation problem). One week later, the children were asked to reproduce what they had seen by drawing the sticks. Only the older children, six to eight years old (and presumably in the Concrete Operational Period), tended to draw an ordered array of sticks. The five-year-olds drew unseriated lines, although the precursors of seriation could be seen. The three- and four-year-olds drew completely unseriated lines. Although memory accuracy was thus correlated with age, the evidence is weak because operational level was not tested in each child; it was merely presumed.

The second type of evidence shows memory to be better after a lapse of time compared with immediate memory. Piaget and Inhelder (1973) retested the children described above eight months after the children had first seen the sticks. The drawings improved in the direction of increased seriation for 74 percent of the children, while the remaining 26 percent did not change. This result has been replicated by other researchers, but children's drawings have also shown increasing amounts of seriation even when a random (nonseriated) array of sticks was the original stimulus to be remembered (see Liben, 1977, for a review).

The third type of evidence that ought to be the strongest support for the Piagetian position would show a relationship between operational level and memory performance for individual children, not just for broad age groups. Unfortunately, the data produced from several different studies do not justify that conclusion at this time. Liben (1977) summarized these studies by saying,

> The Genevan position is undermined by the fact that performance on the two measures has been only weakly related, has occasionally been strikingly asynchronous (for example, children with poor performance on the operative task and perfect performance on the reproduction tasks), and has

not changed in parallel over the long-term retention interval.
[P. 328]

Finally, Flavell and Wellman (1977) noted a similarity between the Soviet view on memory, Piaget's view of knowledge
acquisition, and their own speculations about how metamemory might develop. The Soviet position is that children learn
about memory because they note the relationships between
the original material, their own storage and retrieval attempts,
and the final recalled product (Smirnov, 1973). Piaget proposed
a process, called *reflective abstraction,* which Flavell and Wellman interpreted as follows:

> The child abstracts and permanently incorporates into his
> cognitive structure generalizations or regularities concerning
> the properties of his own actions vis-à-vis the environment.
> [Flavell & Wellman, 1977, pp. 29-30]

They speculate that

> since metamemory . . . primarily [entails] generalizations
> about people and their actions vis-à-vis objects, a process
> like reflective abstraction may play an important role in [its]
> acquisition. [P. 30]

HYPOTHESIS TESTING

Because Formal Operational thinking is the epitome of systematic hypothesis testing, it is reasonable to expect considerable overlap between the types of hypotheses children use in
Levine's blank trials procedure and their level of cognitive
development in Piaget's system. Gholson (1980) has interpreted
Piaget's theory as predicting that Preoperational children
should exhibit only stereotyped responses, never strategies.
Furthermore, because Concrete Operational children neither
consider multiple hypotheses simultaneously nor test hypotheses fully systematically, they should be limited to hypothesis

checking and dimension checking strategies. Only Formal Operational children should exhibit the focusing strategy. As reported in Chapter 3, the general development patterns found on Levine's blank trials problem fit this prediction. Kindergarten children exhibited stereotypes, elementary school children exhibited the two checking strategies with little focusing, and college students focused about half the time. Unfortunately, in those studies, the operational level of individual children was not directly measured. A study which did assess operational level produced confirming evidence (Gholson, O'Connor, & Stern, 1976). Preoperational and Concrete Operational children, all of whom were in kindergarten, were compared on a series of six blank trial problems. The Concrete Operational children solved about 30 percent of the problems; the Preoperational children solved fewer than 10 percent. On a subset of the problems, the Concrete Operational children showed a 35 percent rate of dimension checking and about 10 percent hypothesis checking, whereas the Preoperational children showed less than 10 percent of the two checking strategies combined.

Several training studies have tried to improve children's hypothesis testing (see a review by Tumblin & Gholson, 1981). In each case, children who are in the higher Piagetian stage showed more improvement than their same-aged peers in a lower Piagetian stage. The type of training also makes a difference in the amount of improvement. In fact, the type of training can account for larger performance differences than Piagetian level produces. So, although cognitive level and hypothesis testing are related, the relationship is modified by procedural features of the task (Tumblin & Gholson, 1981).

SUMMARY

Piaget's theory and the process approach are fairly similar in a number of major ways. Both take an interactionist stance, assume that children come to play an active role in their own development, and advocate a moderate novelty principle. Piaget's theory of perception is an enrichment theory, so it contrasts most strongly with Gibson's differentiation theory but agrees with other enrichment theorists. Piaget's work in memory emphasized how the child's general world knowledge and level of cognitive development interact with what is stored in memory. This same position is adopted by Soviet researchers and is compatible with the levels of processing approach. Within the multistore model, those who emphasize the influence of general world knowledge are most similar to Piaget in focus, although they do not necessarily characterize children's world knowledge according to Piaget's stages. Finally, Piaget's description of Concrete and Formal Operational thinking resembles the description of hypothesis generation and hypothesis testing of the process approach.

The major discrepancies between the two theories center on the presence or absence of superordinate cognitive structures and whether developmental change is qualitative as well as quantitative. Piaget's theory is fundamentally a stage theory, proposing qualitative changes and cognitive structures (schemes and operations). Process approach researchers tend to adopt nonstage theories, challenging the idea of superordinate structures (especially operations) and arguing that developmental change tends to be quantitative.

5

IMPLICATIONS FOR PARENTS AND TEACHERS

IMPLICATIONS FOR PARENTING

Since the focus of this book has been on cognitive development rather than socialization, this section on parenting will not discuss such traditional parental concerns as toilet training and sibling rivalry. Instead, we hope to convey a sense of how to enjoy children by watching their cognitive development. While most grandparents expect to receive news when their grandchild sits up alone, cuts a first tooth, and crawls, they do not expect letters or phone calls relating to such milestones as coordinating secondary reactions or searching for hidden objects. Although these cognitive achievements are more difficult to observe, they can be just as exciting and rewarding for parents (and grandparents). Moreover, we hope the focus on cognitive development will present alternative interpretations for some potentially irritating child behaviors. Recall the example from Piaget's fifth stage in the Sensorimotor Period in which children repeatedly drop toys out of their playpens. While one could easily think that the children were maliciously attempting to annoy their caregivers, the alternative explanation offered

157

here was that the dropping activity was essential practice of tertiary circular reactions.

The material in this section is organized around the broad age groups of infants, preschoolers, elementary school children, and adolescents. This is convenient because adults use age as a reference marker, often to judge whether children are acting "normally" and to know what behavior or level of performance to expect from them. This organization is not intended to deny the individual differences between children. Rather, it just reminds us that children are perceived both as individuals and as members of an age group. This same distinction is made by parents in judging their own children's actions. When their child is behaving nicely, parents offer the explanation that their love and gentle guidance produced a well-mannered child. When their child misbehaves, "he is going through a stage" or "acting like all the other 2-year-olds" (or 10-year-olds or adolescents).

One of the major themes of this section is that enjoyment is produced when challenging cognitive tasks are solved, and frustration is produced when a task proves too difficult. Children are confronted with challenging cognitive tasks every day. They have to figure out how their world functions. For parents, the challenging task is to figure out how children function. The purpose of this section is to illuminate the parents' task.

INFANCY

Everyone knows that babies enjoy playing peek-a-boo. For many adults, it is sufficient to know that baby can be amused temporarily by this game. To understand why babies enjoy it, we can examine the development of object permanence. It is a cognitive challenge for infants to figure out that objects can hide temporarily and then reappear. When such an interesting object as a mother hides and reappears, often with a smiling or playful expression on her face, infants can exercise their ideas of object permanence in an enjoyable context.

The development of object permanence can also explain situations of distress for infants. Consider the situation where a six- or seven-month-old infant has been playing happily by himself. Suddenly he begins to cry. The toy that he had held in his hand is on the floor behind his back. One might correctly suspect that his crying resulted from the frustration of not being able to find the "hidden" toy. Returning the toy to his line of vision will bring instant relief. The development of object permanence can also be related to separation anxiety which, as most parents know, is the intense distress infants exhibit when left in an unfamiliar room or with an unfamiliar person. In many instances, infants do not even seem to differentiate between mother's leaving the living room to go to the kitchen and her leaving for the evening. They still wail at the separation. People, being like objects to the infant, acquire a permanence of existence, so when they disappear, the infant may become upset if they cannot be found or made to reappear.

As soon as infants leave the immobility of their first few months and begin to creep, crawl, or walk, literally a whole new world becomes available to them. Prior to self-initiated traveling, the world for infants is severely limited to those objects that parents bring close to them. After they can navigate around the house or yard, and in spite of their parents' best efforts to babyproof the environment, they will undoubtedly get into something dangerous or forbidden. As a result, they are required to learn distinctions between permissible and forbidden activities. The difficulty for infants is that similar actions do not bring similar parental responses.

Parents generally believe that baby grasping a doll or an adult's finger is cute; baby grasping a knife, however, is dangerous. Baby reaching for a bottle will get smiles of encouragement; baby reaching for a full glass will get scolded. Baby pulling on a string attached to a toy is playing; baby pulling on a cord attached to a lamp is in trouble. From the parents' perspective, baby is alternately angelic and mischievous. From the baby's perspective, parents are alternately benevolent and malevolent. Certainly parents must teach their children which activities are permitted and which are not, but they should not be surprised that the discriminations are difficult ones for the children to make. Piaget suggested that the first classification of objects is made according to what schemes can be applied to them. Lamp cords and toy cords are both objects to be pulled, so children classify them together. By forbidding the pulling of lamp cords and permitting the pulling of toy cords, parents require their children to reclassify the objects along a different dimension. The more dimensions of difference between the two objects, the more likely that children will find one that allows them to avoid the forbidden activity. Even then, they might make the discrimination on an incorrect basis. For example, if a child decides that lamp cords are forbidden because they are brown in color whereas toy cords are permissibly white, he will successfully avoid pulling on the lamp until his parents purchase a new lamp with a white cord.

THE PRESCHOOL YEARS

A three-year-old boy drags his mother to the kitchen, opens the oven door, places his hands inside, brings them out again, and extends his arms toward his mother. Smiling, he says, "Want a cookie, Mommy?" His hands are empty. During the Preoperational Period, especially in the preschool years from three to five, children engage in a considerable amount of fantasy play. The world of make-believe is made possible because the Preoperational child has acquired the ability to use symbols. Symbols and language free children's thinking from the immediately perceptible and permit children to express their thoughts and to use their imaginations.

It is not a girl's vivid imagination, however, that leads her to complain about her share of dessert. If her brother's piece of pie is shorter but wider than her own, she may well believe that she got shortchanged. Similarly, once she mashes an unwanted pile of vegetables with her fork, she resists eating them all the more because the pile has gotten larger. Judging from the conservation training research, mere verbal explanations about the equality of the desserts or the unchanged quantity of vegetables are unlikely to change the preschooler's mind. It may well be simpler for a parent to cut the girl's dessert in two, so she believes she now has more, or to repile the vegetables so she believes she now has less.

With the rapid acquisition of language and concepts comes an unceasing interest in how things function, where they come from, and what they are called. "What that?" and "Why?" are nearly as frequently heard as "No, me do it!" Before parents can answer the preschooler's questions, they must figure out what was asked. That is not as easy as it might seem, as we are reminded by the familiar joke about a boy who asked where he came from. After receiving a long explanation about human reproduction from an embarrassed parent, he said, "But Johnny comes from Ohio. Where do I come from?" Elkind (1981) has suggested that young children tend to ask questions about psychological causality although the inquiries might appear to concern physical causes. A typical four-year-old might ask, "Why is the grass green?" or "Why do birds sing?" The answers that are satisfying involve psychological interpretations: the grass is green so it will look pretty; birds sing because they are happy.

In answering children's questions, it is best to remember Grandmother's sage advice to explain events in a child's own language. Even then, though, it is likely that the information will be distorted, as the process of assimilation adjusts the information to the child's current knowledge base. For example, Bernstein and Cowan (1975) reported on children's explanations of where babies come from. One child said, "They just get a duck or a goose and they get a little more growned . . . and then they turn into a baby. . . . They give them some food, people food, and they grow like a baby" (p. 87). A book read to that child about animal and human reproduction was probably too complex for the child to understand. The information about babies was assimilated into more familiar terms: ducks hatch from eggs, and feeding people helps them grow.

Perception is quite well developed in preschoolers, although they need a more complete stimulus than older children do in order to identify an object correctly. A closet door is therefore likely to become a monster as soon as the bedroom light is turned off because the partial stimulus which remains visible is not sufficient to be a convincing closet door. Moreover, showing these children that the monster is gone when the light is turned on is not persuasive. They, unlike infants, have object permanence, so the monster can easily reappear in the dark; just because they cannot see it in the light does not mean it is gone forever.

The highly limited deliberate memory abilities of preschoolers mean that they should not be expected to remember everything they have been asked to do, especially if the list is long. Face and hands might be washed, but ears are forgotten. If an interesting toy is lying in front of Father's slippers, Father's feet might get very cold as he waits for the child to remember the errand. These apparent disadvantages of preschoolers' memories are offset because they are also likely to forget some treat that had been promised by a harried parent. Distraction from a forbidden activity still works if the distractor is highly attractive, but this technique is not as successful as it is for infants. Finally, hypothesis testing will seem like unsystematic, idiosyncratic guessing rather than any pattern that could be called strategic or systematic. This might be seen in preschoolers' ideas about how a new story might end, where their shoes have been left, where pieces fit into a new puzzle, or how to fix a broken toy. The correct solution might be found, but only by trial and error.

THE ELEMENTARY SCHOOL YEARS

To many observers, the elementary school years are relatively quiet ones, especially because children do not need as much monitoring as preschoolers and infants. School, of course, absorbs a good deal of time as does playing games. We will look at school activity in the educational implications section, so the focus here will be on the impact of cognitive development on children's games.

We have already seen that the game of Twenty Questions exercises children's skills of hypothesis testing and that Concentration games exercise rote memory. Card games are also popular at this age, providing practice with numbers and classification. In gin rummy, for example, a number (e.g., 6) can be part of a run (5, 6, 7) or it can be part of a set of 6's, one from each suit. The child who can classify both ways and keep both possibilities in mind simultaneously will do better than the child who fixes on one classification and ignores the other. Memory is important as children try to keep track of what discards have been made and how these affect the possible plays in their own hands. They can develop hypotheses about which cards are likely to benefit their opponents. They can practice arithmetic skills in calculating the score. Frequently children will exhibit an unwarranted satisfaction with the one hypothesis they have generated instead of a thoughtful consideration of many alternative solutions, and their hypothesis testing will begin to be more systematic, but not fully efficient.

When a game can be played in many different ways, children of a wide variety of ages can enjoy it, although the older child or adult, with multiple strategies, is likely to be a better player. Consider an anagram game in which a set of letters is rearranged to form as many words as possible. A young child's strategy might be to think of a word and then see if it can be spelled with the available letters. Another strategy is to pick several letters at random and try to combine them in several orders. After the child has worked with this subset for a while, the letters can be returned to the pile and another subset drawn. A third strategy is to search for those letter combinations which are more frequent in the language as root words. Although these strategies differ considerably in their sophistication and probability for success, even young elementary schoolers can play the game with enjoyment.

If parents believe it possible to analyze their children's strategies, it is likely to occur to them that they could try to teach their children the more advanced strategies.* Two questions, however, should be raised: Can the parents teach the strategies? Should they try? The first is an empirical question. Depending on their ability to analyze the child's current level of functioning and to teach the more advanced strategies in a way that is meaningful to him, some parents will experience success. The second question is a philosophical one. What are the costs and benefits of teaching? The costs can be measured in time and motivation. If children are led to believe that their way of playing a game is wrong or stupid, and if they experience any difficulty in learning the correct or smart way, they are simply likely to avoid playing. The game will cease to be fun. If, on the other hand, they learn quickly and painlessly, the benefits may be satisfaction in solving a problem in a new manner and the competitive advantage of knowing a better way to play. Obviously no hard-and-fast rules can be made about whether or not to intervene.

ADOLESCENCE

Parents of elementary school children see that time as the lull before the storm. Adolescence is often as welcome as a sore

---

* Indeed, the search for training paradigms that accelerate children's acquisition of a particular skill seems to be a preoccupation among American researchers, educators, and parents. Piaget found this theme to recur so often that he labeled it "the American Question."

tooth because the stereotyped view of the period is as a time of rapid change, of social and sexual identity crises, of replacing parental values for peer values. That the stereotype is true for only a minority of adolescents has not weakened parental fears. Against such a background, the cognitive advances of the adolescent may not seem welcome either, for as we have already seen, Formal Operational adolescents are likely to appear argumentative as they examine their old beliefs in sets and discover inconsistencies. Profound shock awaits the unsuspecting parent who suddenly is confronted by a series of why questions: "Why can't I drink, smoke, or engage in sex?" "Why do I have to attend school or church?" "Why do I have to be home at midnight?" These why questions are much different from the four-year-old's. The psychological interpretations that satisfied the preschooler are obviously not going to please adolescents. They need detailed, factual information, often including rationalizations, for why they must engage in certain activities, especially if adults are not required to do so. Parents should expect charges of hypocrisy if their responses to their adolescents are not satisfactory.

SUMMARY

This section has offered suggestions for analyzing various problem situations and recommended that parents create their own list of solutions. The analysis that children drop food from their highchairs because of circular reactions is not advice on how to cope with the situation. Some parents will spread a plastic cloth on the floor and let their children drop as much as they please. Other parents will feed their children, denying them access to the food. Still others will ask their children to make a distinction between dropping toys, which is acceptable, and dropping food, which is not. Since most problems have a variety of potential solutions, the only real difficulty is finding one which is acceptable to parents and within the child's capability.

Unfortunately, that ideal is not always easy to meet. One

such episode occurred when a father asked me for advice on how to stop his two-year-old daughter from eating his cigarettes. I asked him to analyze the situation from her perspective. First, she watches him put cigarettes into his mouth. Imitation is a highly probable response, especially considering her age. Since she has no experience with smoking, she probably assimilates the activity into the more familiar eating scheme. The problem her father would like her to solve is a discrimination between his smoking, which she should not imitate, and his eating, which she should. That distinction may be too difficult to make. Secondly, the cigarettes are easily accessible on the coffee table. Because they are rather novel, she has a high motivation to investigate them, including shredding them and tasting them. Furthermore, she is allowed to pull apart and taste other items, especially food, that are given to her on that same coffee table. Again, the discrimination she is being asked to make is a difficult one.

Although I suggested that the father either give up smoking or at least keep his cigarettes out of her reach, for example, on the fireplace mantle, he insisted that she needed to learn the discrimination he had set up and rejected the idea that she might be too immature (both cognitively and emotionally) to learn it. Although the distinctions between eating and smoking and between eating food and eating cigarettes would be trivially easy to learn when she was a few years older, this father seemed to believe that only his solution (that the daughter be taught the distinctions now) was correct. I concluded that he was probably still in the Concrete Operational Period and resolved to stop giving advice.

EDUCATIONAL IMPLICATIONS

THE PROCESS APPROACH

The experimental tradition of process approach research includes constructing experimental tasks which resemble academic tasks, with modifications to make them "pure" measures of one or another process or subprocess. The extent to which experimental conclusions can then be applied back to classrooms has never been very clear. When process approach researchers talk about educational implications at all, it tends to be in the form of broad recommendations rather than specific curriculum suggestions. The simple fact that processes are studied in isolation from each other indicates that process approach researchers will not be well equipped to discuss how to put all the pieces together, as a teacher must do. Nevertheless, it is useful to look at the recommendations because they can remind the educator where to look when difficulties arise in the educational process.

Attention

No matter what task is set before children, it is a truism that they must direct attention to the task. In the earlier grades, especially, directed attention is itself a difficult task for children. Characteristics of the stimulus array can make some features so compelling that children cannot avoid looking at them (and hence fail to attend to the more relevant but less interesting features), or the entire task may be so uncompelling as to attract too little attention compared with the diversions any child can find around a classroom. Consider a book aimed at teaching young children to read. If the different letters in each word are printed in bright colors, the children might not attend sufficiently to the shapes of the letters, which distinguish them. If interesting pictures are printed opposite the words, children might prefer to look at the pictures. On the other hand, with no pictures or colors, children may not be attracted to the book at all.

Perception

The most extensive application of perception research has been in the area of reading, with Gibson's differentiation theory having the strongest influence (Williams, 1979). Yet after several decades of intensive reading research, we still do not have a clear picture of either the reading process or the best curriculum for teaching reading. Gibson and Levin (1975) concluded that "the reading process is rule governed and incapable of adequate description in simple terms" (p. 482). The rules which they believe govern reading are the same as those which govern perceptual development. Readers learn to select out the relevant information, ignore the irrelevant, and search for information efficiently. Selecting relevant information means that the distinctive features of letters (e.g., straight vs. curved lines, open vs. closed features) must be identified. Irrelevant information which can usually be ignored includes type font and color (except when they are used for emphasis). Visual scanning strategies refer to the control over eye movements so that (in English) words are read from left to right, preventing mistakes such as reading *saw* for *was*.

Learning to scan a page in the proper direction is sufficiently challenging that children practice it spontaneously. Elkind and Weiss (1967) demonstrated this when they asked children to name pictures that were arranged in a triangular pattern. Five-year-olds (probably not yet readers) and eight-year-olds (probably adequate readers) named the pictures by starting at the top and following around the triangular outline. Many of the young readers (six and seven years old) named the pictures from left to right, top to bottom. This was clearly a less efficient scanning strategy that was applied inappropriately, but it provided practice on a skill that was being learned. (Such spontaneous practice fits nicely with Piaget's idea that schemes are applied across many contexts merely because they are available to be exercised.) The broader implication is that teachers should be alert to the possibility that poor performance on one task may result from children's spontaneous practice of a skill they are learning in a different context.

Two other principles from perception that apply in reading are that readers will learn to process larger units of information and that they will process the least amount of information that still yields meaning. Part of the skill readers acquire is to read whole words instead of individual letters and phrases instead of individual words. The other principle means that they learn to use the many redundancies available to reduce the strain on the information processing system. Redundancies occur at many levels in reading. (a) At the level of individual letters, more than one distinctive feature helps to distinguish between letters. For example, the letter *R* is different from *E* by being curved, not straight; closed, not open; and unsymmetrical (Gibson, 1970). (b) Positions that letters may take within words are restricted. For example, *ck* is acceptable in English at the end of a word but not at the beginning. (c) Positions of words within sentences are constrained by what has come before them in the sentence. For example, after the article *the,* only a noun or adjective may follow, not a verb. (d) Words are limited by the gist of the sentence and paragraph. For example, "lightning" can "strike," but it cannot "sit." (For a more detailed analysis of redundancies, see Haber, 1978.)

Theories of perception have generally been cited as support for a phonics approach to teaching reading, under the argument that children need to learn to decode the letter patterns into sounds and to attach meanings to the sounds. The alternative position, that reading should be taught by a whole-word or sight-recognition method, is more likely to look for support in memory research.

Memory

Memory research dealing with how general world knowledge influences current information processing is applicable to the problem of reading. Whenever children encounter a new word, they can guess from the gist of the passage what that word might be. It is not uncommon for the beginning reader to come upon the following passage, "The dog said woof-woof," and read instead, "The dog said arf-arf" because prior exposure to dogs (and stories) supplied an incorrect inference about the last word. Another intrusion of prior knowledge into reading occurred when the young son of a physician laughed and said, "There's a doctor named Ugs." The sign he had read was "Drugs," but he had interpreted it as "Dr. Ugs" in keeping with his familiarity with doctors. Perhaps most importantly, though, memory is required in reading because the reader must remember the first part of a sentence while processing the last part in order to make sense of the whole thing. Many beginning readers read so slowly that they exceed their own memory spans. Each word in a sentence may be read accurately, but the words are not put together into a meaningful whole.

Although the phonics approach is frequently portrayed as the opposite of the whole-word approach, in curriculum design both are incorporated, and the debate really concerns the balance between the two. The levels of processing view of memory supports the position that both semantic and sensory analyses are needed, and in fact cannot really be separated. As Lockhart (1979) said,

> There is a tendency to regard the sensory components of a word or a picture as a kind of detachable skin within which is the kernel of meaning but that itself is meaningless. Sensory and semantic features do not possess this simple additive relationship. The sensory codes are aspects of analysis of meaning. [P. 82]

Broad recommendations stemming from memory research can be applied to nearly any educational task, not just reading. In the early grades, especially, when deliberate memory is poorly developed, teachers can work directly on improving it by teaching strategies and by teaching children to monitor their own memory efforts (Brown & DeLoache, 1978). Campione and Brown (1977) suggested teaching children to match their memory strategy to the task. Rehearsal should be used when the amount of information to be remembered is small and when verbatim (exact) recall is needed. An organizing strategy should

170

be used when material has an inherent organization (not necessarily hierarchical) or when idiosyncratic organizations can be imposed by the child. Elaborative rehearsal is the preferred strategy when initially unrelated items must be associated (e.g., names and dates in history) and when a sufficient amount of study time is allowed.

Alternatively, as long as deliberate memory remains weak, educators can take advantage of involuntary memory by embedding memory in other meaningful tasks. The Soviets advocate a type of discovery learning to replace rote memorization. For example, Smirnov and Zinchenko (1969) recommended having children generate multiplication tables (repeatedly if necessary) instead of being given the tables to memorize directly. In the same way that general world knowledge was useful in reading, it will be useful in any school task where comprehension is desired. Understanding, and also remembering, will be automatic to the extent that new information is compatible with a child's existing knowledge (Brown, 1979).

Hypothesis testing

Hypothesis testing of the type discussed in the process approach section is directly relevant in courses where scientific reasoning is used (e.g., high school science courses) or where logical inferences are made about causes and effects (e.g., literature, history, geometry). In the earlier grades, hypotheses are still generated and tested, but children are less systematic and efficient at doing so, and the content in elementary school courses rarely calls for these skills.

A simpler kind of hypothesis generation can be seen in the rules which children acquire, especially in language and arithmetic. As was discussed earlier, children are expected to learn major rule systems, such as the grammar of their language, without formal instruction before they get to school. In school, however, teachers must correct any misconceptions children have about grammar rules and teach the more obscure rules

171

directly. Children generate rules in other contexts on an informal basis, often in unexpected ways. One beginning reader, for example, showed me how she was to sound out the name of several pictures and circle the ones which matched the ending sound of a target word. She offered the "advice" that usually two of the four pictures were matches, but sometimes "they try to fool you and only one picture is correct." Her hypothesis was, in fact, a good one. Every set of pictures did have two which were supposed to match. Sometimes she found fewer matches because of incorrectly identifying the pictures (she called a horn a trumpet and so did not match it to the *corn* target word). It is not at all clear that her teacher would have wanted her to use the number of pictures already circled as a factor in her decision about what to circle, but the teacher can use such knowledge to diagnose the child's errors.

At other times, children can solve problems without knowing a general rule to cover the cases. One child announced to his astonished math teacher that he knew when numbers were even or odd, but only up to 999. It was frightening to think that he must have memorized each number separately instead of learning a rule to look at the last digit.

Concepts

Children might have difficulty learning if some concepts are too abstract, too complex, or lack status or validity. When children's sense of time is not fully developed, they will have as much trouble conceptualizing ancient Roman battles as the Vietnam War. Although their teacher may have vivid personal memories of the latter, the children will not, so both historical times will be difficult for them to learn. The succession of English kings or American presidents are lists to be learned by rote, since children have few personal experiences with kings or presidents. In fact, younger children's concepts of political systems and governments can be characterized as personalized, concrete, and incomplete (Adelson & O'Neil, 1966). When asked the function of taxes, for example, 11-year-olds tended to reply, "to pay for the police," whereas an 18-year-old might say, "to run the government." The younger children's answers deal with highly visible services. Adolescents refer to less visible, more abstract functions; they know that there is more to government than just police or fire services.

PIAGET'S THEORY

It is easy to understand why educators hoped Piaget's theory would easily lead to specific curriculum suggestions. Despite criticisms of one or another of its aspects, the theory is the most comprehensive for intellectual development. It potentially addresses all levels of education, provides a goal to reach (Formal Operational thinking), and gives a broad timetable for reaching that goal. Consequently, educators have used the theory descriptively, by adopting Piagetian terminology to explain children's educational difficulties, and prescriptively, by setting goals and methods of education compatible with the theory.

Assimilation and accommodation

The concepts of assimilation and accommodation are particularly valuable in summarizing what children do in educational situations. Ginsburg (1977) demonstrated both concepts in the context of arithmetic. Assimilation explains why children convert the teacher-given problem into one more familiar to them, such as by changing multiplication into repeated addition. When children are learning to write large numbers, the command to write "forty-two" may produce an answer like "402," because the written system for numbers is assimilated into the spoken system. Accommodation can be seen in children's invented procedures for solving novel problems. A third grader who could do column addition correctly "solved" a new, linear addition problem as follows: $52 + 123 + 4 = 17$. The accommodation was to ignore place values (thus changing the old way of doing addition) and to add each digit individually. Kamii (1973) described the impact of assimilation and accommodation for teachers: "What we think we are teaching and what the child actually learns may turn out to be two different things" (p. 224).

Content of instruction

The first attempts to use Piaget's theory prescriptively resulted in new curriculum content aimed at moving children from one stage of development to another. Three experimental programs, all designed to change preschool children to the Concrete Operational Period, were developed in the early 1970s (Kamii, 1972; Lavatelli, 1970; Weikart, Rogers, Adcock, & McClelland, 1971). These were soon abandoned, in part because researchers decided no clear rationale existed for trying to make children attain Concrete Operations earlier than they usually did (Kuhn, 1979). At the high school level, one program has been developed to teach Formal Operational thinking in the context of biology (Lawson, 1975). Evaluation of it is hampered, however, by the difficulties in assessing Formal Operations outside of Piaget and Inhelder's original set of tasks (Kuhn, 1979).

Educators have shifted away from using Piaget's stage theory to set the content of the curriculum. DeVries (1978) expressed one reason for this: "By focusing on the stages which are the *result* of development, one misses entirely the theme of Piaget's theory—constructivism—which deals with the *process* of development" (p. 77, italics in original). Instead, educational objectives are now phrased in terms of children's mental activities and social relations. Kamii and DeVries (1977), for example, set two cognitive and three socio-emotional goals for a preschool program, which include having children generate interesting ideas, problems, and questions and notice the relationships among objects. Similarly, the "thinking games" described by

174

Furth and Wachs (1975) reflect the goals of thinking and creativity over more narrowly defined skills and factual knowledge. Educators appeal to Piaget's stage theory to argue (a) for allowing children to move from one wrong answer to another rather than from a wrong answer to the "adult" right answer and (b) for permitting them time to consolidate their gains before asking them to make new advances (Elkind, 1971; Kamii, 1973).

Methods of instruction

To derive recommendations about how teachers should teach, educational researchers have looked at various aspects of Piaget's theory. This occasionally results in conflicting advice (Murray, 1979). Generally, Piaget's theory is seen as compatible with open education, discovery learning, and Montessori's methods, because they all emphasize the self-initiated activity of the learner (Murray, 1978). In a discovery approach to spelling, for example, Duckworth (1973) recommended that children generate all possible ways for writing the sounds of the words. Thus, to spell the word *cousin,* children can suggest *c* or *k, ou* or *oo, s* or *z,* and so on. After all the alternatives are suggested, teachers can point out the usual way. Duckworth noted, "Instead of feeling stupid for creating an unconventional spelling, the children feel clever. . . . They also know . . . that there is only one correct way to write any given word" (1973, p. 152). Yet Elkind (1971) criticized discovery learning because it tries to stimulate a child's intrinsic motivation to learn by manipulating task characteristics rather than by giving the child more control over the learning environment, such as providing large blocks of time in areas of interest to him. Furthermore, Brainerd (1978) criticized discovery learning in general, and Piaget's version of it for training conservation in particular, because tutorial methods were more efficient and more likely to work with a broader sample of children.

Good and Brophy (1980) suggested that Piaget's theory is compatible with discovery learning only for the upper elementary and high school levels. Discovery learning encourages children to act mentally and physically on objects in order to discover their properties and the relationships between them. This utilizes "operative" knowing and so is only appropriate for Concrete and Formal Operational children, corresponding to the upper elementary and high school grades. In contrast, Preoperational thinking is "figurative," involving copying or reproducing the environment rather than changing it. At the preschool and early elementary grades, children are more likely to be in the Preoperational Period. Therefore, the traditional early school tasks of copying alphabet letters and memorizing simple vocabulary and arithmetic facts are more compatible with Piaget's theory for early education.

Piaget's theory has also been viewed as compatible with Montessori's methods for preschool education. Both agree that children's motivation to learn is intrinsic, and so both advocate child-initiated activities. Learning during the Preoperational Period is largely physical, rather than verbal, so children should be given many opportunities to interact with material physically. To learn about numbers, children need objects to count. To learn about colors, children can sort colored objects, not just recite names while teachers hold up colored swatches. To learn shapes, they can place shapes in a form board, copy designs, or walk patterns on a floor. Yet Piaget (1969) rejected the Montessori materials when used alone, on the grounds that the materials were too structured and too focused on sensory learning.

Two other aspects of learning which Piaget and Montessori both stressed are repetition and imitation. The need for repetition is seen in Piaget's theory in the principle of organization. Schemes and operations must be practiced in order to make them function more smoothly and efficiently. Since teachers cannot see inside a child's head to determine whether a structure is well-organized, they must allow each child freedom to practice and to set an individual pace to learning. Montessori

(1964, 1967; Rambusch, 1962) also recommended that children be allowed to set their own pace but warned that they might stay with a well-rehearsed skill after they are ready to move on if they are afraid of failing the next task or if no new task is available. Teachers, therefore, should have new material ready for introduction and then observe the children for signs of the proper moment to present it. Kamii (1973) warned of the difficulty in finding the right balance between intruding too much on the child's activity and being too passive.

In addition to repetition, imitation is an important tool in learning, as is readily observable in preschool children. Montessori and Piaget believed in exploiting this tendency by allowing children the freedom to move around the classroom and to observe other children's activities. In many cases, a child might provide a better model than an adult for how to perform some task. If the child uses intermediate steps toward the solution that an adult might skip, or if the child's relatively poor dexterity requires a different movement than the adult would make, then a child model will be better. Children are also more likely to exhibit incorrect problem-solving strategies which the observing child can then avoid.

The recommendation to encourage imitation can be misinterpreted in two ways, both of which the reader is cautioned against. First, it does not mean that one particular child is identified as a star and held up as an example to the other children. No child wants to be reprimanded with "Why can't you behave as well as sweet little Johnny?" The imitation described by Montessori and Piaget is spontaneous in the sense of being child-initiated. It springs from the observing child's desire to acquire the skill displayed by the other child. Second, the recommendation for imitation should not be construed as a rejection of the importance of individual differences or creativity. Learning is paced by each child and conducted according to a unique set of needs and prior experiences. The purpose of imitation is not to create similarity among children. Rather, it is to foster the learning of skills that would be accomplished more slowly through direct tuition or through trial-and-error learning.

Since the kind of imitation that Piaget suggested was child-initiated, his followers and collaborators have not exploited observational learning as a method of accelerating or teaching cognitive skills such as conservation. Instead, they have consistently advocated a type of discovery learning in which the teacher helps induce conflicts between what a child predicts might happen and what actually does happen (Inhelder, Sinclair, & Bovet, 1974). Brainerd's (1978) criticism is again appropriate here, because experimenter-directed observational learning (exposing, say, a nonconserving child to a model of another child who does conserve) is an effective training procedure according to some research.

Kamii and DeVries (1977, 1978) suggested that a teacher's methods for implementing the curriculum should correspond to the type of knowledge to be acquired. Piaget (1969) distinguished between three types of knowledge: physical, logico-mathematical, and social-arbitrary. Physical knowledge concerns the physical properties of objects and what can be done to them. Children discover these properties for themselves when they act on the objects. For example, they discover which objects float and which objects sink by placing them in water. They blow on objects through a straw to find out if that will move them across the floor. Logico-mathematical knowledge involves the child's actions on objects, not the objects themselves. For example, knowledge that the same number results when a row is counted from left to right as from right to left is derived from the counting activity, not from any property of the object counted. For both physical and logico-mathematical knowledge, the teacher does not need to provide feedback or reinforcement for learning to occur. What teachers do need to do is provide situations where the actions can take place and encourage the children to engage in the activity. For example, if children help prepare a table for eating a snack, they can count the plates, cups, and napkins each time they place an object on the table. Thus, for these two types of knowledge, a form of discovery learning is recommended.

The third category, social-arbitrary knowledge, is transmitted by the culture and includes the arbitrary rules governing interpersonal relations. Learning to take turns, to clean up after playing, and to throw balls but not blocks are examples of social-arbitrary knowledge. This information is taught directly by teachers and by other children and should be reinforced because motivation to learn these rules is not intrinsic to any situation or object. Thus many aspects of the traditional preschool curriculum are suitable for stimulating intellectual development, but the teacher's role varies according to the situation (and the child).

Most of the curriculum and method suggestions made so far have been aimed at the preschool level. This undoubtedly reflects the fact that researchers have much more ready access to preschool classrooms and fewer restrictions in implementing curriculum changes. Nevertheless, some suggestions are applicable to any grade level. Duckworth (1979) pointed out that any classroom is bound to have enormous variations in children's level of development and that designing individual programs for each child is virtually impossible. She recommended that teachers "offer situations in which children at various levels, whatever their intellectual structures, can come to know parts of the world in a new way" (p. 311). Gallagher (1981) encouraged teachers to look to Piaget's principles of assimilation and accommodation in order to decide what questions to ask children during a reading lesson. While some factual questions are necessary, teachers can also ask questions which suggest a new perspective or which prompt the children to integrate their personal experiences with facts in the story. Both Gallagher (1978) and DeVries (1978) cautioned against the common superficial application of Piagetian theory that merely gives children physical objects to manipulate. "These applications are not inconsistent with . . . Piaget's theory. Nevertheless, they have the effect of reducing it to a pale shadow of Piaget's meaning" (DeVries, 1978, p. 79).

It should be obvious by now that the connection between Piaget's theory and educational practices is far from clear. Three major reasons for this have been offered. First, Piaget studied laws of development which would have universal application; traditional American education, in contrast, is concerned with individual differences, not universality (Sigel, 1978). Second, Piaget was not concerned directly with education. His interests were in the development of knowledge, not the acquisition of skills and factual information (Murray, 1979; Sigel, 1978). Third, the theory still has major ambiguities. Kuhn (1979) identified the two most important: (a) the cognitive competencies associated with each stage are not fully specified and (b) the method for recognizing when a child is "cognitively active" is unknown.

> To the extent that developmental stages are not fully defined, the recommendation that curriculum be based on them becomes an empty one. . . . The need [is] to define . . . the nature of self-directed intellectual activity and the process by which it becomes developmentally transformed. Without such knowledge, there is no basis on which to substantiate the assertion that the ideal educational environment is one in which students are allowed to choose and direct their own activities. [Kuhn, 1979, p. 358]

SUMMARY

This chapter has indicated in a general fashion how Piaget's theory and the process approach can be useful to parents and educators. The philosophy expressed in both the parenting and educational sections was that children are fundamentally different from adults; therefore, what seems reasonable from an adult's perspective may be unreasonable from a child's point of view, and vice versa. Both previous experience and current cognitive knowledge put limits on what children can learn. Sometimes those limitations are demonstrated when the child misbehaves; other times, the limitations show as a failure to profit from classroom instruction.

The characteristics of the Piagetian stages and the developmental advances in the processes of thought provide clues to parents concerning the reasons for their child's behavior. Many actions which are annoying might be slightly more tolerable if parents could figure out what problems their children are trying to solve. Teachers were also encouraged to analyze the tasks they demand of their pupils. Successful learning is more likely to occur if the problem is within the child's perceptual, memory, and hypothesis testing skills. Moreover, the problems are more likely to be solved if their elements are familiar to children and if they are presented concretely rather than abstractly, at least for the elementary school and preschool child.

Finally, the connection between Piagetian theory and educational practice is not straightforward. While it is generally seen as compatible with discovery learning approaches, educators have varied considerably in their interpretations of how the theory is to be implemented.

REFERENCES

Acredelo, L. P., Pick, H. L., Jr., & Olsen, M. G. Environmental differentiation and familiarity as determinants of children's memory for spatial location. *Developmental Psychology*, 1975, *11*, 495-501.

Adelson, J., & O'Neil, R. P. Growth of political ideas in adolescence: The sense of community. *Journal of Personality and Social Psychology*, 1966, *4*, 295-306.

Allik, J., & Valsiner, J. Visual development in ontogenesis: Some reevaluations. In H. W. Reese & L. P. Lipsitt (Eds.), *Advances in child development and behavior* (Vol. 15). New York: Academic Press, 1980.

Arlin, P. K. Cognitive development in adulthood: A fifth stage? *Developmental Psychology*, 1975, *11*, 602-606.

Atkinson, K., MacWhinney, B., & Stoel, C. *An experiment on the recognition of babbling.* Papers and reports on child language development. Committee on Linguistics, Stanford University, 1970, No. 1.

Atkinson, R. C., & Shiffrin, R. M. Human memory: A proposed system and its control processes. In K. W. Spence & J. T. Spence (Eds.), *The psychology of learning and motivation* (Vol. 2). New York: Academic Press, 1968.

Ault, R. L. Problem-solving strategies of reflective, impulsive, fast-accurate, and slow-inaccurate children. *Child Development*, 1973, *44*, 259-266.

Beilin, H. *Piaget and the new functionalism.* Address to the Eleventh Symposium of the Jean Piaget Society, Philadelphia, May 1981.

Bernstein, A. C., & Cowan, P. A. Children's concepts of how people get babies. *Child Development*, 1975, *46*, 77-91.

Bower, T. G. R. The object in the world of the infant. *Scientific American*, 1971, *225*, 30-38.

Brainerd, C. J. Learning research and Piagetian theory. In L. S. Siegel & C. J. Brainerd (Eds.), *Alternatives to Piaget: Critical essays on the theory.* New York: Academic Press, 1977.

Brainerd, C. J. *Piaget's theory of intelligence.* Englewood Cliffs, N.J.: Prentice-Hall, 1978.

Brainerd, C. J., & Allen, T. W. Experimental inductions of the conservation of "first-order" quantitative invariants. *Psychological Bulletin*, 1971, *75*, 128-144.

Brainerd, C. J., & Brainerd, S. H. Order of acquisition of number and quantity conservation. *Child Development*, 1972, *43*, 1401-1406.

Brekke, B., Williams, J. D., & Tait, P. The acquisition of conservation of weight by visually impaired children. *Journal of Genetic Psychology*, 1974, *125*, 89-97.

Brown, A. L. The development of memory: Knowing, knowing about knowing, and knowing how to know. In H. W. Reese (Ed.), *Advances in child development and behavior* (Vol. 10). New York: Academic Press, 1975.

Brown, A. L. Theories of memory and the problems of development: Activity, growth and knowledge. In L. S. Cermak & F. I. M. Craik (Eds.), *Levels of processing in human memory.* Hillsdale, N.J.: Lawrence Erlbaum, 1979.

Brown, A. L., & DeLoache, J. S. Skills, plans, and self-regulation. In R. S. Siegler (Ed.), *Children's thinking: What develops?* Hillsdale, N.J.: Lawrence Erlbaum, 1978.

Bruner, J. S. On perceptual readiness. *Psychological Review,* 1957, *64,* 123-152.

Bruner, J. S., Olver, R. R., & Greenfield, P. M. *Studies in cognitive growth.* New York: Wiley, 1966.

Caldwell, E. C., & Hall, V. C. Distinctive-features versus prototype learning reexamined. *Journal of Experimental Psychology,* 1970, *83,* 7-12.

Campione, J. C., & Brown, A. L. Memory and metamemory development in educable retarded children. In R. V. Kail, Jr., & J. W. Hagen (Eds.), *Perspectives on the development of memory and cognition.* Hillsdale, N.J.: Lawrence Erlbaum, 1977.

Chi, M. T. H. Short-term memory limitations in children: Capacity or processing deficits? *Memory and Cognition,* 1976, *4,* 559-572.

Chi, M. T. H. Knowledge structures and memory development. In R. S. Siegler (Ed.), *Children's thinking: What develops?* Hillsdale, N.J.: Lawrence Erlbaum, 1978.

Cohen, L. B. A two process model of infant visual attention. *Merrill-Palmer Quarterly,* 1973, *19,* 157-180.

Cohen, L. B. Our developing knowledge of infant perception and cognition. *American Psychologist,* 1979, *34,* 894-899.

Cohen, L. B., DeLoache, J. S., & Strauss, M. S. Infant visual perception. In J. D. Osofsky (Ed.), *Handbook of infant development.* New York: Wiley, 1979.

Cohen, L. B., & Gelber, E. R. Infant visual memory. In L. B. Cohen & P. Salapatek (Eds.), *Infant perception: From sensation to cognition* (Vol. 1). New York: Academic Press, 1975.

Cohen, L. B., Gelber, E., & Lazar, M. Infant habituation and generalization to differing degrees of stimulus novelty. *Journal of Experimental Child Psychology,* 1971, *11,* 379-389.

Cowan, P. A. *Piaget: With feeling.* New York: Holt, Rinehart and Winston, 1978.

Craik, F. I. M. Levels of processing: Overview and closing comments. In L. S. Cermak & F. I. M. Craik (Eds.), *Levels of processing in human memory.* Hillsdale, N.J.: Lawrence Erlbaum, 1979.

Craik, F I. M., & Lockhart, R. S. Levels of processing: A framework for memory research. *Journal of Verbal Learning and Verbal Behavior,* 1972, *11,* 671-684.

Dasen, P. R. (Ed.). *Piagetian psychology: Cross-cultural contributions.* New York: Gardner Press, 1977.

Day, M. C. Developmental trends in visual scanning. In H. W. Reese (Ed.), *Advances in child development and behavior* (Vol. 10). New York: Academic Press, 1975.

DeVries, R. Early education and Piagetian theory. In J. M. Gallagher & J. A.

Easley, Jr. (Eds.), *Knowledge and development* (Vol. 2). New York: Plenum, 1978.

Duckworth, E. Language and thought. In M. Schwebel & J. Raph (Eds.), *Piaget in the classroom.* New York: Basic Books, 1973.

Duckworth, E. Either we're too early and they can't learn it or we're too late and they know it already: The dilemma of "Applying Piaget." *Harvard Educational Review,* 1979, *49,* 297-312.

Elkind, D. Two approaches to intelligence: Piagetian and psychometric. In D. R. Green, H. P. Ford, & G. B. Flamer (Eds.), *Measurement and Piaget.* New York: McGraw-Hill, 1971.

Elkind, D. Perceptual development in children. *American Scientist,* 1975, *63,* 533-541.

Elkind, D. *Children and adolescents: Interpretive essays on Jean Piaget* (3rd ed.). New York: Oxford University Press, 1981.

Elkind, D., & Weiss, J. Studies in perceptual development III: Perceptual exploration. *Child Development,* 1967, *38,* 1153-1161.

Ennis, R. H. Conditional logic and primary school children: A developmental study. *Interchange,* 1971, *2,* 126-132.

Flavell, J. H. *The developmental psychology of Jean Piaget.* Princeton, N.J.: Van Nostrand, 1963.

Flavell, J. H. First discussant's comments: What is memory development the development of? *Human Development,* 1971, *14,* 272-278.

Flavell, J. H. *Cognitive development.* Englewood Cliffs, N.J.: Prentice-Hall, 1977.

Flavell, J. H., Beach, D. R., & Chinsky, J. M. Spontaneous verbal rehearsal in a memory task as a function of age. *Child Development,* 1966, *37,* 283-299.

Flavell, J. H., Friedrichs, A. G., & Hoyt, J. D. Developmental changes in memorization processes. *Cognitive Psychology,* 1970, *1,* 324-340.

Flavell, J. H., & Wellman, H. M. Metamemory. In R. V. Kail, Jr., & J. W. Hagen (Eds.), *Perspectives on the development of memory and cognition.* Hillsdale, N.J.: Lawrence Erlbaum, 1977.

Furth, H. G. *Piaget and knowledge.* Englewood Cliffs, N.J.: Prentice-Hall, 1969.

Furth, H. G., & Wachs, H. *Thinking goes to school: Piaget's theory in practice.* New York: Oxford University Press, 1975.

Gallagher, J. M. Reflexive abstraction and education. In J. M. Gallagher & J. A. Easley, Jr. (Eds.), *Knowledge and development* (Vol. 2). New York: Plenum, 1978.

Gallagher, J. M. *Training teachers in the understanding of inferences: A Piagetian perspective.* Paper presented at the Eleventh Symposium of the Jean Piaget Society, Philadelphia, May 1981.

Geis, M. F., & Hall, D. M. Encoding and incidental memory in children. *Journal of Experimental Child Psychology,* 1976, *22,* 58-66.

Geis, M. F., & Hall, D. M. Encoding and congruity in children's incidental memory. *Child Development,* 1978, *49,* 857-861.

Gelman, R. Conservation acquisition: A problem of learning to attend to relevant attributes. *Journal of Experimental Child Psychology,* 1969, *7,* 167-187.

Gelman, R. Cognitive development. In M. R. Rosenzweig & L. W. Porter (Eds.), *Annual review of psychology* (Vol. 29). Palo Alto: Annual Reviews, Inc., 1978.

Gelman, R. Why we will continue to read Piaget. *The Genetic Epistemologist,* 1979, *8*(4), 1-3.

Gholson, B. *The cognitive-developmental basis of human learning: Studies in hypothesis testing.* New York: Academic Press, 1980.

Gholson, B., & Beilin, H. A developmental model of human learning. In H. W. Reese & L. P. Lipsitt (Eds.), *Advances in child development and behavior* (Vol. 13). New York: Academic Press, 1979.

Gholson, B., O'Connor, J., & Stern, I. Hypothesis sampling systems among preoperational and concrete operational kindergarten children. *Journal of Experimental Child Psychology,* 1976, *21,* 61-76.

Gibson, E. J. *Principles of perceptual learning and development.* New York: Appleton-Century-Crofts, 1969.

Gibson, E. J. The development of perception as an adaptive process. *American Scientist,* 1970, *58,* 98-107.

Gibson, E. J., & Levin, H. *The psychology of reading.* Cambridge, Mass.: MIT Press, 1975.

Ginsburg, H. *Children's arithmetic: The learning process.* New York: Van Nostrand, 1977.

Ginsburg, H., & Opper, S. *Piaget's theory of intellectual development.* Englewood Cliffs, N.J.: Prentice-Hall, 1979.

Gleitman, L. *What some concepts might not be.* Invited address to the Eleventh Symposium of the Jean Piaget Society, Philadelphia, May 1981.

Glick, J. *Culture and cognition: Some theoretical and methodological concerns.* Paper presented at the American Anthropological Association Meetings, New Orleans, November 1969.

Gollin, E. S. Developmental studies of visual recognition of incomplete objects. *Perceptual and Motor Skills,* 1960, *11,* 289-298.

Gollin, E. S. Factors affecting the visual recognition of incomplete objects: A comparative investigation of children and adults. *Perceptual and Motor Skills,* 1962, *15,* 583-590.

Good, T. L., & Brophy, J. E. *Educational psychology: A realistic approach.* New York: Holt, Rinehart and Winston, 1980.

Gratch, G. Recent studies based on Piaget's view of object concept development. In L. B. Cohen & P. Salapatek (Eds.), *Infant perception: From sensation to cognition* (Vol. 2). New York: Academic Press, 1975.

Greenfield, P. M. Cross-cultural research and Piagetian theory: Paradox and progress. In K. F. Riegel & J. A. Meacham (Eds.), *The developing individual in a changing world.* Chicago: Aldine, 1976.

Gruber, H. E., Girgus, J. S., & Banuazizi, A. The development of object permanence in the cat. *Developmental Psychology,* 1971, *4,* 9-15.

Gruen, G. E., & Vore, D. A. Development of conservation in normal and retarded children. *Developmental Psychology,* 1972, *6,* 146-157.

Haber, R. N. Visual perception. In M. R. Rosenzweig & L. W. Porter (Eds.), *Annual review of psychology* (Vol. 29). Palo Alto: Annual Reviews, Inc., 1978.

Hagen, J. W. Development and models of memory: Comments on the papers by Brown and Naus and Halasz. In L. S. Cermak & F. I. M. Craik (Eds.), *Levels of processing in human memory.* Hillsdale, N.J.: Lawrence Erlbaum, 1979.

Hagen, J. W., & Stanovich, K. G. Memory: Strategies of acquisition. In R. V. Kail, Jr., & J. W. Hagen (Eds.), *Perspectives on the development of memory and cognition.* Hillsdale, N.J.: Lawrence Erlbaum, 1977.

Hoving, K. L., Spencer, T., Robb, K. Y., & Schulte, D. Developmental changes in visual information processing. In P. A. Ornstein (Ed.), *Memory development in children.* Hillsdale, N.J.: Lawrence Erlbaum, 1978.

Inhelder, B., & Piaget, J. *The growth of logical thinking from childhood to adolescence* (trans. A. Parsons & S. Milgram). New York: Basic Books, 1958.

Inhelder, B., Sinclair, H., & Bovet, M. *Learning and the development of cognition* (trans. S. Wedgwood). Cambridge, Mass.: Harvard University Press, 1974.

Jacoby, L. L., & Craik, F. I. M. Effects of elaboration of processing at encoding and retrieval: Trace distinctiveness and recovery of initial context. In L. S. Cermak & F. I. M. Craik (Eds.), *Levels of processing in human memory.* Hillsdale, N.J.: Lawrence Erlbaum, 1979.

Jeffrey, W. E. The orienting reflex and attention in cognitive development. *Psychological Review,* 1968, *75,* 323-334.

Jensen, A. R. How much can we boost IQ and scholastic achievement? *Harvard Educational Review,* 1969, *39,* 1-123.

Jensen, A. R. Cumulative deficit in IQ of blacks in the rural south. *Developmental Psychology,* 1977, *13,* 184-191.

Kagan, J. A conception of early adolescence. *Daedalus,* 1971, *100,* 997-1012.

Kagan, J., Klein, R. E., Haith, M. M., & Morrison, F. J. Memory and meaning in two cultures. *Child Development,* 1973, *44,* 221-223.

Kagan, J., Rosman, B. L., Day, D., Albert, J., & Phillips, W. Information processing in the child: Significance of analytic and reflective attitudes. *Psychological Monographs,* 1964, *78* (1, Whole No. 578).

Kail, R. V., Jr., & Siegel, A. W. The development of mnemonic encoding in children: From perception to abstraction. In R. V. Kail, Jr., & J. W. Hagen (Eds.), *Perspectives on the development of memory and cognition.* Hillsdale, N.J.: Lawrence Erlbaum, 1977.

Kamii, C. An application of Piaget's theory to the conceptualization of a preschool curriculum. In M. C. Day & R. K. Parker (Eds.), *The preschool in action.* Boston: Allyn & Bacon, 1972.

Kamii, C. Piaget's interactionism and the process of teaching young children. In M. Schwebel & J. Raph (Eds.), *Piaget in the classroom.* New York: Basic Books, 1973.

Kamii, C., & DeVries, R. Piaget for early education. In M. C. Day & R. K.

Parker (Eds.), *The preschool in action* (2nd ed.). Boston: Allyn & Bacon, 1977.

Kamii, C., & DeVries, R. *Physical knowledge in preschool education: Implications of Piaget's theory.* Englewood Cliffs, N.J.: Prentice-Hall, 1978.

Keeney, T. J., Cannizzo, S. R., & Flavell, J. H. Spontaneous and induced verbal rehearsal in a recall task. *Child Development,* 1967, *38,* 953-966.

Kesner, R. P., & Baker, T. B. Neuroanatomical correlates of language and memory: A developmental perspective. In R. L. Ault (Ed.), *Developmental perspectives.* Santa Monica: Goodyear, 1980.

Kingsley, P. R., & Hagen, J. W. Induced versus spontaneous rehearsal in short-term memory in nursery school children. *Developmental Psychology,* 1969, *1,* 40-46.

Kodroff, J., & Roberge, J. Developmental analysis of the conditional reasoning abilities of primary-grade children. *Developmental Psychology,* 1975, *11,* 21-28.

Kolers, P. A. A pattern-analyzing basis of recognition. In L. S. Cermak & F. I. M. Craik (Eds.), *Levels of processing in human memory.* Hillsdale, N.J.: Lawrence Erlbaum, 1979.

Kreutzer, M. A., Leonard, C., & Flavell, J. H. An interview study of children's knowledge about memory. *Monographs of the Society for Research in Child Development,* 1975, *40* (1, Serial No. 159).

Kuczaj, S. A., II. Children's judgments of grammatical and ungrammatical irregular past-tense verbs. *Child Development,* 1978, *49,* 319-326.

Kuhn, D. The application of Piaget's theory of cognitive development to education. *Harvard Educational Review,* 1979, *49,* 340-360.

Kumler, H. *Primate societies: Group techniques of ecological adaptation.* Chicago: Aldine-Atherton, 1971.

Lavatelli, C. S. *Piaget's theory applied to an early childhood curriculum.* Boston: American Science & Engineering, 1970.

Lawson, A. Developing formal thought through biology teaching. *American Biology Teacher,* 1975, *37,* 411-429.

Levine, M. Hypothesis behavior by humans during discrimination learning. *Journal of Experimental Psychology,* 1966, *71,* 331-338.

Levine, M., Leitenberg, H., & Richter, M. The blank trials law: The equivalence of positive reinforcement and nonreinforcement. *Psychological Review,* 1964, *71,* 94-103.

Lewis, M., & Brooks, J. Infants' social perception: A constructivist view. In L. B. Cohen & P. Salapatek (Eds.), *Infant perception: From sensation to cognition* (Vol. 2). New York: Academic Press, 1975.

Liben, L. S. Memory in the context of cognitive development: The Piagetian approach. In R. V. Kail, Jr., and J. W. Hagen (Eds.), *Perspectives on the development of memory and cognition.* Hillsdale, N.J.: Lawrence Erlbaum, 1977.

Lockhart, R. S. Remembering events: Discussion of papers by Jacoby and Craik, Battig, and Nelson. In L. S. Cermak & F. I. M. Craik (Eds.), *Levels of processing in human memory.* Hillsdale, N.J.: Lawrence Erlbaum, 1979.

Lockhart, R. S., Craik, F. I. M., & Jacoby, L. L. Depth of processing, recognition and recall. In J. Brown (Ed.), *Recall and recognition*. New York: Wiley, 1976.

Lovell, K. Some aspects of the work of Piaget in perspective. In A. Floyd (Ed.), *Cognitive development in the school years*. New York: Halsted, 1979.

Markman, E. M., & Siebert, J. Classes and collections: Internal organization and resulting holistic properties. *Cognitive Psychology*, 1976, *8*, 561-577.

McCall, R. B. Attention in the infant: Avenue to the study of cognitive development. In D. Walcher & D. Peters (Eds.), *Early childhood: The development of self-regulatory mechanisms*. New York: Academic Press, 1971.

McLaughlin, G. H. Psychologic: A possible alternative to Piaget's formulation. *British Journal of Educational Psychology*, 1963, *33*, 61-67.

Meacham, J. A. Soviet investigations of memory development. In R. V. Kail, Jr., & J. W. Hagen (Eds.), *Perspectives on the development of memory and cognition*. Hillsdale, N.J.: Lawrence Erlbaum, 1977.

Mervis, C. B., & Rosch, E. Categorization of natural objects. In M. R. Rosenzweig & L. W. Porter (Eds.), *Annual review of psychology* (Vol. 32). Palo Alto: Annual Review, Inc., 1981.

Millar, S. Spatial representations by blind and sighted children. *Journal of Experimental Child Psychology*, 1976, *21*, 460-479.

Miller, G. A. The magical number seven, plus or minus two: Some limits on our capacity for processing information. *Psychological Review*, 1956, *63*, 81-97.

Milne, A. A. *The house at Pooh Corner*. New York: Dutton, 1961. (a)

Milne, A. A. *Winnie-the-Pooh*. New York: Dutton, 1961. (b)

Mitchell, C., & Ault, R. L. *The development of involuntary memory*. Paper presented at the Southwestern Regional Society for Research in Human Development. Lawrence, Kan., March 1980.

Moely, B., Olson, P. A., Halwes, T. G., & Flavell, J. H. Production deficiency in young children's clustered recall. *Developmental Psychology*, 1969, *1*, 26-34.

Montessori, M. *Dr. Montessori's own handbook*. Cambridge, Mass.: Bentley, 1964.

Montessori, M. *The Montessori method* (trans. A. E. George). Cambridge, Mass.: Bentley, 1967.

Mosher, F. A., & Hornsby, J. R. On asking questions. In J. S. Bruner, R. R. Olver, & P. M. Greenfield (Eds.), *Studies in cognitive growth*. New York: Wiley, 1966.

Murray, F. B. Two models of human behavior and reading instruction. In J. M. Gallagher & J. A. Easley, Jr. (Eds.), *Knowledge and development* (Vol. 2). New York: Plenum, 1978.

Murray, F. B. The future of Piaget's theory in education. *The Genetic Epistemologist*, 1979, *8*(4), 7-10.

Mussen, P. H., Conger, J. J., Kagan, J., & Geiwitz, J. *Psychological development: A life-span approach*. New York: Harper & Row, 1979.

Naus, M. J., & Halasz, F. G. Developmental perspectives on cognitive processing and semantic memory structure. In L. S. Cermak & F. I. M. Craik

(Eds.), *Levels of processing in human memory.* Hillsdale, N.J.: Lawrence Erlbaum, 1979.

Naus, M. J., Ornstein, P. A., & Hoving, K. L. Developmental implications of multistore and depth-of-processing models of memory. In P. A. Ornstein (Ed.), *Memory development in children.* Hillsdale, N.J.: Lawrence Erlbaum, 1978.

Neimark, E. Intellectual development during adolescence. In F. D. Horowitz (Ed.), *Review of child development research* (Vol. 4). Chicago: University of Chicago Press, 1975.

Neisser, U. The control of information pickup in selective looking. In A. D. Pick (Ed.), *Perception and its development.* Hillsdale, N.J.: Lawrence Erlbaum, 1979.

Olver, R. R., & Hornsby, J. R. On equivalence. In J. S. Bruner, R. R. Olver, & P. M. Greenfield (Eds.), *Studies in cognitive growth.* New York: Wiley, 1966.

Ornstein, P. A., Naus, M. J., & Liberty, C. Rehearsal and organizational processes in children's memory. *Child Development,* 1975, *46,* 818-830.

Owings, R. A., & Baumeister, A. A. Levels of processing, encoding strategies, and memory development. *Journal of Experimental Child Psychology,* 1979, *28,* 100-118.

Paris, S. G. Comprehension of language connectives and propositional logical relationships. *Journal of Experimental Child Psychology,* 1973, *16,* 278-291.

Paris, S. G., & Lindauer, B. K. The role of inference in children's comprehension and memory for sentences. *Cognitive Psychology,* 1976, *8,* 217-227.

Paris, S. G., & Lindauer, B. K. Constructive aspects of children's comprehension and memory. In R. V. Kail, Jr., & J. W. Hagen (Eds.), *Perspectives on the development of memory and cognition.* Hillsdale, N.J.: Lawrence Erlbaum, 1977.

Paris, S. G., & Upton, L. R. Children's memory for inferential relationships in prose. *Child Development,* 1976, *47,* 660-668.

Perlmutter, M., & Myers, N. A. Recognition memory development in two- to four-year-olds. *Developmental Psychology,* 1974, *10,* 447-450.

Piaget, J. *Play, dreams, and imitation in childhood* (trans. C. Gattegno & F. M. Hodgson). New York: Norton, 1951.

Piaget, J. *The origins of intelligence in children* (trans. M. Cook). New York: International University Press, 1952.

Piaget, J. *The construction of reality in the child* (trans. M. Cook). New York: Basic Books, 1954.

Piaget, J. The general problems of the psychobiological development of the child. In J. M. Tanner & B. Inhelder (Eds.), *Discussions on child development* (Vol. 4). London: Tavistock, 1960.

Piaget, J. *Science of education and the psychology of the child.* New York: Viking, 1969.

Piaget, J. Piaget's theory. In P. H. Mussen (Ed.), *Carmichael's manual of child psychology* (Vol. 1). New York: Wiley, 1970.

190

Piaget, J. Intellectual evolution from adolescence to adulthood. *Human Development,* 1972, *15,* 1-12.

Piaget, J., & Inhelder, B. *Memory and intelligence* (trans. A. J. Pomerans). New York: Basic Books, 1973.

Piaget, J., & Inhelder, B. The gaps in empiricism. In B. Inhelder & H. Chipman (Eds.), *Piaget and his school.* New York: Springer-Verlag, 1976.

Rambusch, N. M. *Learning how to learn: An American approach to Montessori.* Baltimore: Helicon Press, 1962.

Reese, H. W. Imagery and associative memory. In R. V. Kail, Jr., & J. W. Hagen (Eds.), *Perspectives on the development of memory and cognition.* Hillsdale, N.J.: Lawrence Erlbaum, 1977.

Riegel, K. F. Dialectic operations: The final period of cognitive development. *Human Development,* 1973, *16,* 346-370.

Rosch, E., Mervis, C. B., Gray, W. D., Johnson, D. M., & Boyes-Braem, P. Basic objects in natural categories. *Cognitive Psychology,* 1976, *8,* 382-439.

Santostefano, S., & Paley, E. Development of cognitive controls in children. *Child Development,* 1964, *35,* 939-949.

Scarr-Salapatek, S. Race, social class and IQ. *Science,* 1971, *174,* 1285-1295.

Scarr, S., & Weinberg, R. A. IQ test performance of black children adopted by white families. *American Psychologist,* 1976, *31,* 726-739.

Shepp, B. E., Burns, B., & McDonough, D. The relation of stimulus structure to perceptual and cognitive development: Further tests of a separability hypothesis. In F. Wilkening, J. Becker, & T. Trabasso (Eds.), *Information integration by children.* Hillsdale, N.J.: Lawrence Erlbaum, 1980.

Siegler, R. S. The origins of scientific reasoning. In R. S. Siegler (Ed.), *Children's thinking: What develops?* Hillsdale, N.J.: Lawrence Erlbaum, 1978.

Siegler, R. S. Developmental sequences within and between concepts. *Monographs of the Society for Research in Child Development,* 1981, *46*(2, Serial No. 189).

Sigel, I. E. Introduction. In J. M. Gallagher & J. A. Easley, Jr. (Eds.), *Knowledge and development* (Vol. 2). New York: Plenum, 1978.

Smirnov, A. A. *Problems of the psychology of memory* (trans. S. A. Corson). New York: Plenum, 1973.

Smirnov, A. A., & Zinchenko, P. I. Problems in the psychology of memory. In M. Cole & I. Maltzman (Eds.), *A handbook of contemporary Soviet psychology.* New York: Basic Books, 1969.

Sophian, C., & Hagen, J. W. Involuntary memory and the development of retrieval skills in young children. *Journal of Experimental Child Psychology,* 1978, *26,* 458-471.

Sperling, G. The information available in brief visual presentation. *Psychological Monographs,* 1960, *74*(11, Whole No. 498).

Stevenson, H. W. *Children's learning.* New York: Appleton-Century-Crofts, 1972.

Strauss, S., & Levin, I. Commentary on R. S. Siegler's Developmental sequences within and between concepts. *Monographs of the Society for Research in Child Development,* 1981, *46*(2, Serial No. 189).

191

Stroop, J. R. Studies of interference in serial verbal reactions. *Journal of Experimental Psychology*, 1935, *18*, 643-662.

Trabasso, T., Isen, A. M., Dolecki, P., McLanahan, A. G., Riley, C. A., & Tucker, T. How do children solve class-inclusion problems? In R. S. Siegler (Ed.), *Children's thinking: What develops?* Hillsdale, N.J.: Lawrence Erlbaum, 1978.

Tulving, E., & Thomson, D. M. Encoding specificity and retrieval processes in episodic memory. *Psychological Review*, 1973, *80*, 352-373.

Tumblin, A., & Gholson, B. Hypothesis theory and the development of conceptual learning. *Psychological Bulletin*, 1981, *90*, 102-124.

Uzgiris, I. C. Situational generality of conservation. *Child Development*, 1964, *35*, 831-841.

Van Horn, K. R., & Bartz, W. H. Information seeking strategies in cognitive development. *Psychonomic Science*, 1968, *11*, 341-342.

Vendovitskaya, T. V. Development of memory. In A. V. Zaporozhets & D. B. Elkonin (Eds.), *The psychology of preschool children* (trans. J. Shybut & S. Simon). Cambridge, Mass.: MIT Press, 1971.

Vernon, M. D. The functions of schemata in perceiving. *Psychological Review*, 1955, *62*, 180-192.

Weikart, D., Rogers, L., Adcock, C., & McClelland, D. *The cognitively oriented curriculum*. Urbana, Ill.: ERIC-NAEYE, 1971.

Weir, M. W. Developmental changes in problem-solving strategies. *Psychological Review*, 1964, *71*, 473-490.

Wellman, H. M., Ritter, K., & Flavell, J. H. Deliberate memory behavior in the delayed reactions of very young children. *Developmental Psychology*, 1975, *11*, 780-787.

Williams, J. Reading instruction today. *American Psychologist*, 1979, *34*, 917-922.

Wise, K. L., Wise, L. A., & Zimmermann, R. R. Piagetian object permanence in the infant rhesus monkey. *Developmental Psychology*, 1974, *10*, 429-437.

Youniss, J. Operational development in deaf Costa Rican subjects. *Child Development*, 1974, *45*, 212-216.

Zaporozhets, A. V., & Elkonin, D. B. (Eds.). *The psychology of preschool children* (trans. J. Shybut & S. Simon). Cambridge, Mass.: MIT Press, 1971.

AUTHOR INDEX

SUBJECT INDEX

197